At-Home Tutor
Language
2
Grade 2

I0821687

-ail Word Family

Write the letters on the lines to make **-ail** words.
Then sound out the words you wrote.

1.  p + **ail** ___ ___ ___ ___ (3 under the 2nd line)

2. 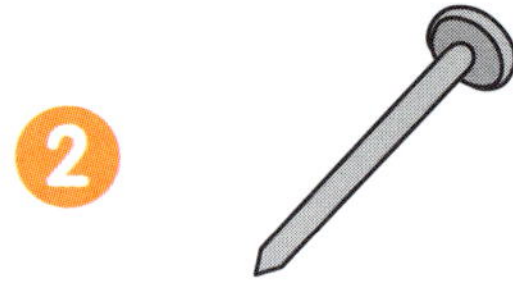 n + **ail** ___ ___ ___ ___ (2 under the 1st line)

3.  m + **ail** ___ ___ ___ ___ (4 under the 3rd line)

4.  s + **ail** ___ ___ ___ ___ (1 under the 1st line, 5 under the 4th line)

Now write each of the numbered letters on the matching lines below.
Read the rhyme.

A slimy ___ ___ ___ ___ ___ will leave a trail.
(lines numbered 1 2 3 4 5)

A Dog and a Snail

Read the poem. Underline the words in the **-ail** family.

I have a sweet dog who likes snails.
He finds one and then wags his tail.
His nose to the ground,
He sniffs all around
And follows their slippery trail.

-ail Pairs

Here are some riddles for you to solve.
The answers will be words in the **-ail** family.

1. a bucket of building supplies

   __________ __________

2. a slow way to get a letter

   __________ __________

3. the end of a special bird

   __________ __________

4. a slippery critter leaves a mark

   __________ __________

-ight Word Family

Write the letters on the lines to make **-ight** words.
Then sound out the words you wrote.

1. 
n + ight ____ ____ ____ ____ ____

(1 under the first line)

2. 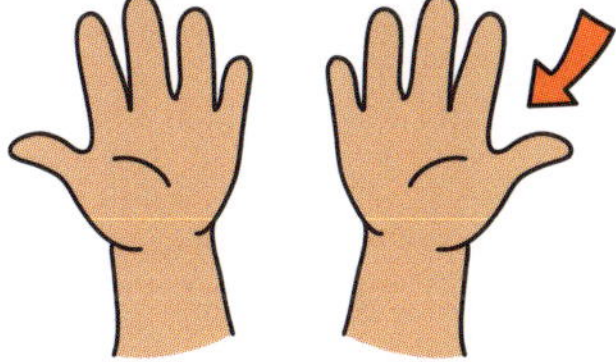
r + ight ____ ____ ____ ____ ____

(2 under the second line)

3. 
l + ight ____ ____ ____ ____ ____

(3 under the third line, 5 under the fifth line)

4. 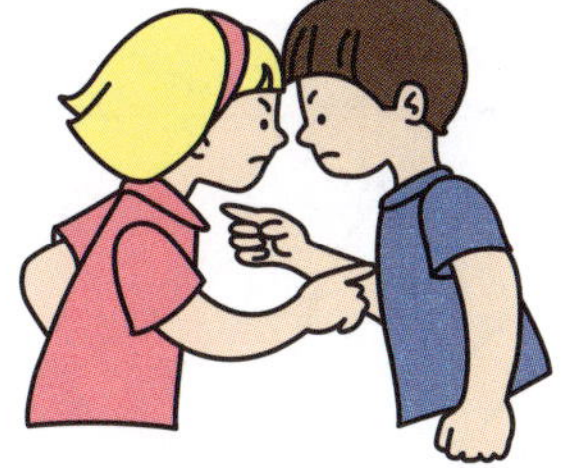
f + ight ____ ____ ____ ____ ____
(4 under the fourth line)

Now write each of the numbered letters on the matching lines below.
Read the rhyme.

Good ____ ____ ____ ____ ____!
1 2 3 4 5

Sleep ____ ____ ____ ____ ____!
5 2 3 4 5

Good Night

Read the poem. Underline the words in the **-ight** family.

There once was a girl from Nepal
Whose room, to her, seemed dark and small.
She thought a night light
Might lessen her fright.
She likes that bright light on her wall!

-ight Pairs

Here are some riddles for you to solve.
The answers will be words in the **-ight** family.

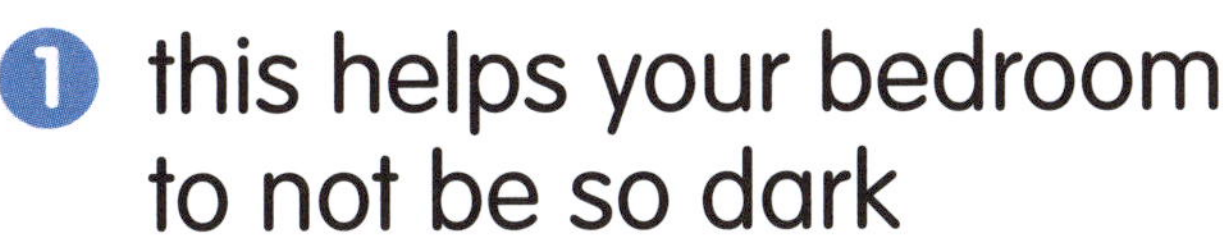

1. this helps your bedroom to not be so dark

   ____________ ____________

2. colorful leg wear

   ____________ ____________

3. armored men in a conflict

   ____________ ____________

4. not the light on the left, but the

   ____________ ____________

-eeze Word Family

Write the letters on the lines to make **-eeze** words.
Then sound out the words you wrote.

1.  br + eeze ______________________

2. 

sn + eeze ______________________

3.  fr + eeze ______________________

4.  squ + eeze ______________________

Now draw something you can **squeeze**.

Wheeze and Sneeze

Read the poem. Underline the words in the **-eeze** family.

I see flowers sway in the breeze.
My eyes water and I start to wheeze.
It's allergy season.
This is the reason
that when I'm outside I will sneeze.

-eeze Words

Look at what the breeze blew in!

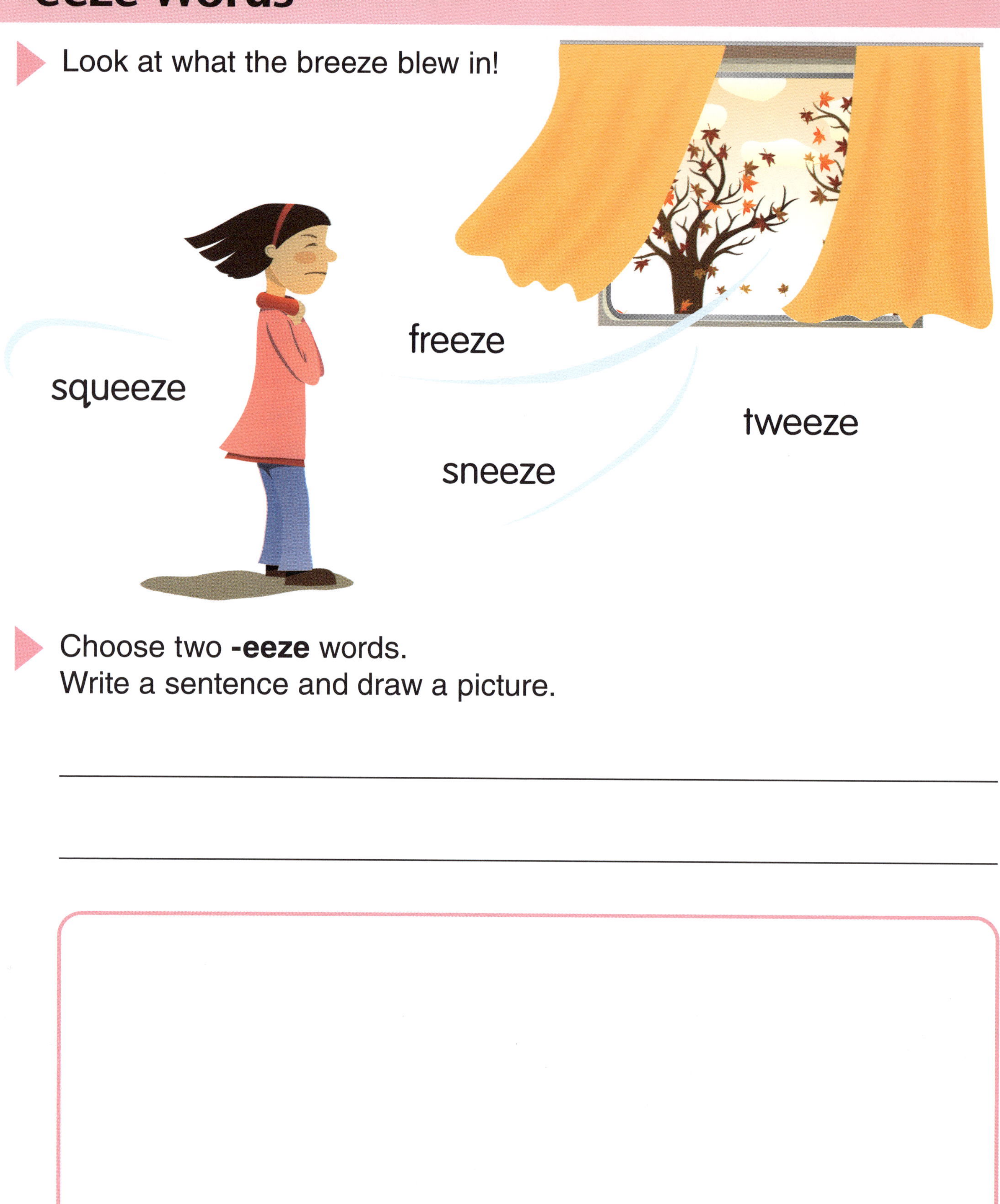

Choose two **-eeze** words.
Write a sentence and draw a picture.

-ound Word Family

Write the letters on the lines to make **-ound** words.
Then sound out the words you wrote.

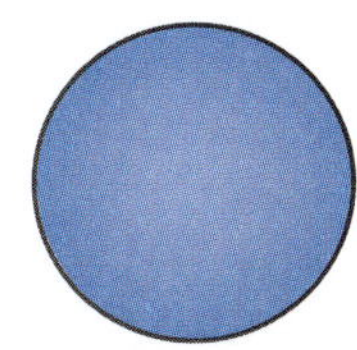

r + **ound** _____ _____ _____ _____ _____

2

2 

h + **ound** _____ _____ _____ _____ _____

3 

s + **ound** _____ _____ _____ _____ _____

4 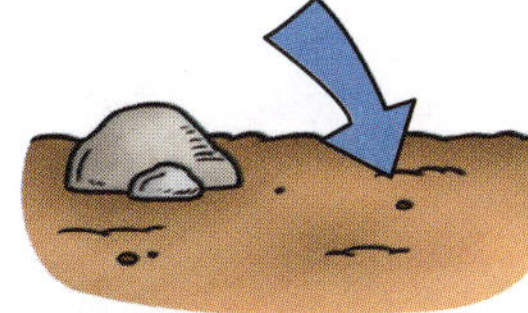

gr + **ound** _____ _____ _____ _____ _____ _____

3

Now write each of the numbered letters on the matching lines below.
Read the rhyme.

This little 

just heard a 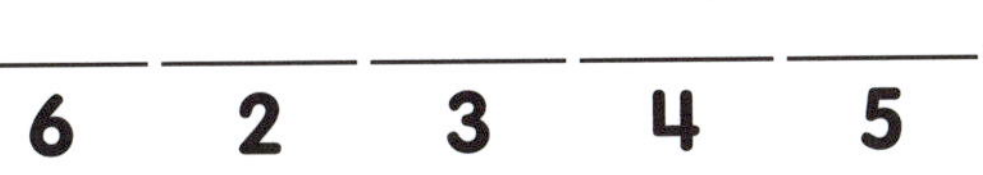.

I Found a Hound

Read the poem. Underline the words in the **-ound** family.

I once found a wonderful hound.
She was just walking around.
We went to the park
And stayed until dark
Taking turns on the merry-go-round.

Pumpkins All Around

Read the poem.
Underline the words in the **-ound** family on the pumpkins.

Pumpkin seeds
So dry and white
Went in the fertile ground.
By and by
A vine emerged
Then out came words with **-ound**!

-own Word Family

Write the letters on the lines to make **-own** words.
Then sound out the words you wrote.

  cr + own 

___ ___ ___ ___ ___
1

  t + own

___ ___ ___ ___
3, 5

3  d + own 

___ ___ ___ ___
4

4  br + own

___ ___ ___ ___ ___
2

Now write each of the numbered letters on the matching lines below.
Read the rhyme.

The queen wore a gown

and a sparkly ___ ___ ___ ___ ___.
1 2 3 4 5

Upside-Down Clown

Read the poem. Underline the words in the **-own** family.

The circus is here in my town.
I laugh at the silly old clown.
He does a handstand.
Now, isn't that grand?
But his smile kind of looks like a frown!

An -own Picture

Find all the **-own** words. Color them **brown**.

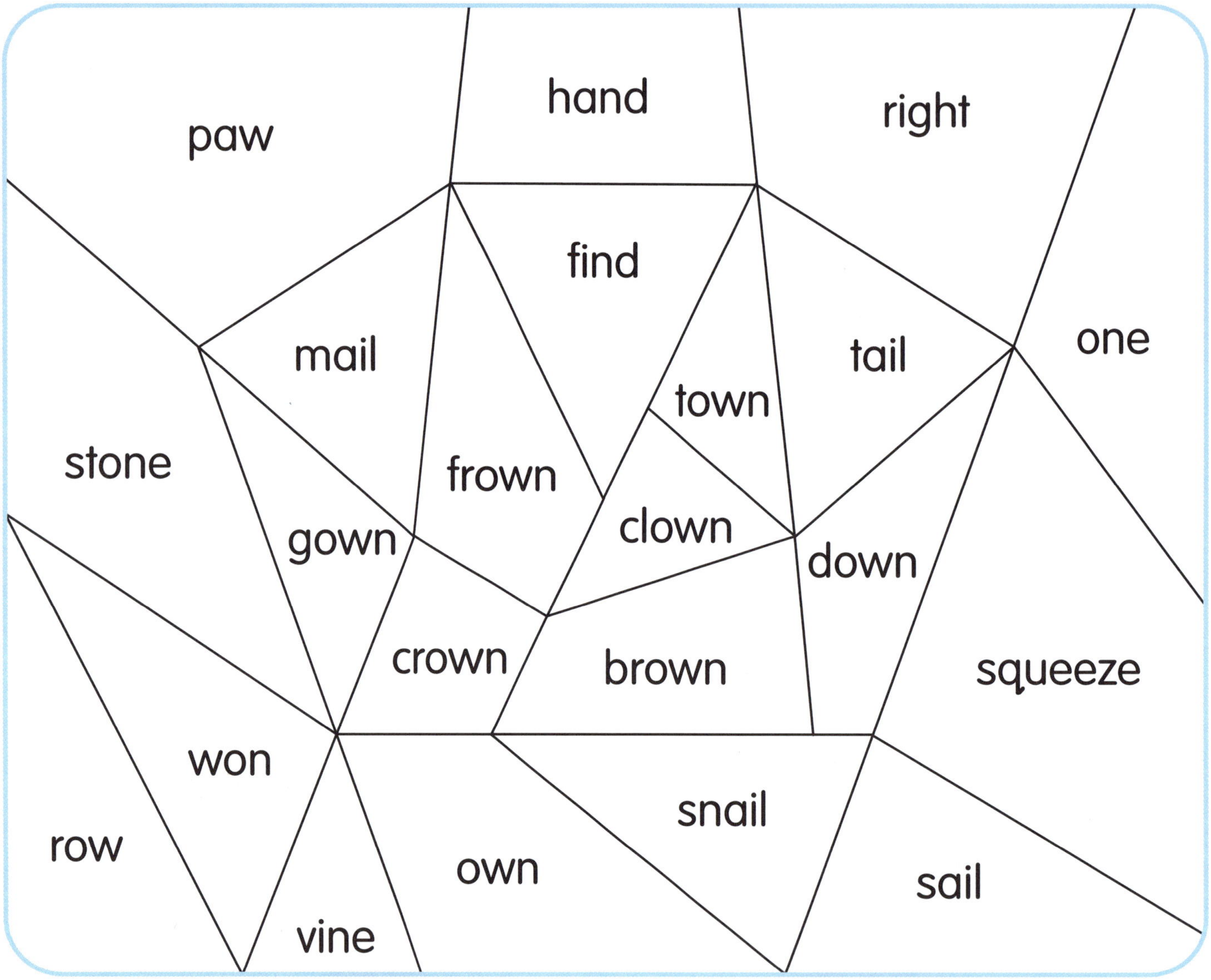

paw hand right
find
mail town tail one
stone frown clown down
gown
crown brown squeeze
won
row snail
own sail
vine

What is it?

A brown ________________

-ore Word Family

Write the letters on the lines to make **-ore** words.
Then sound out the words you wrote.

sc + **ore** ___ ___ ___ ___ ___ (4)

2

st + **ore** ___ ___ ___ ___ ___ (3)

3

sh + **ore** ___ ___ ___ ___ ___ (2)

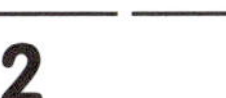

4

c + **ore** ___ ___ ___ ___ (1, 5)

Now write each of the numbered letters on the matching lines below.
Read the rhyme.

Sweeping the floor

is my daily ___ ___ ___ ___ ___.

1 2 3 4 5

Lenore the Dancer

Read the poem. Underline the words in the **-ore** family.

Such a great dancer is Lenore.

I like the pink tutu she wore.

Her ankle is sore.

But look at that score!

She danced better than ever before.

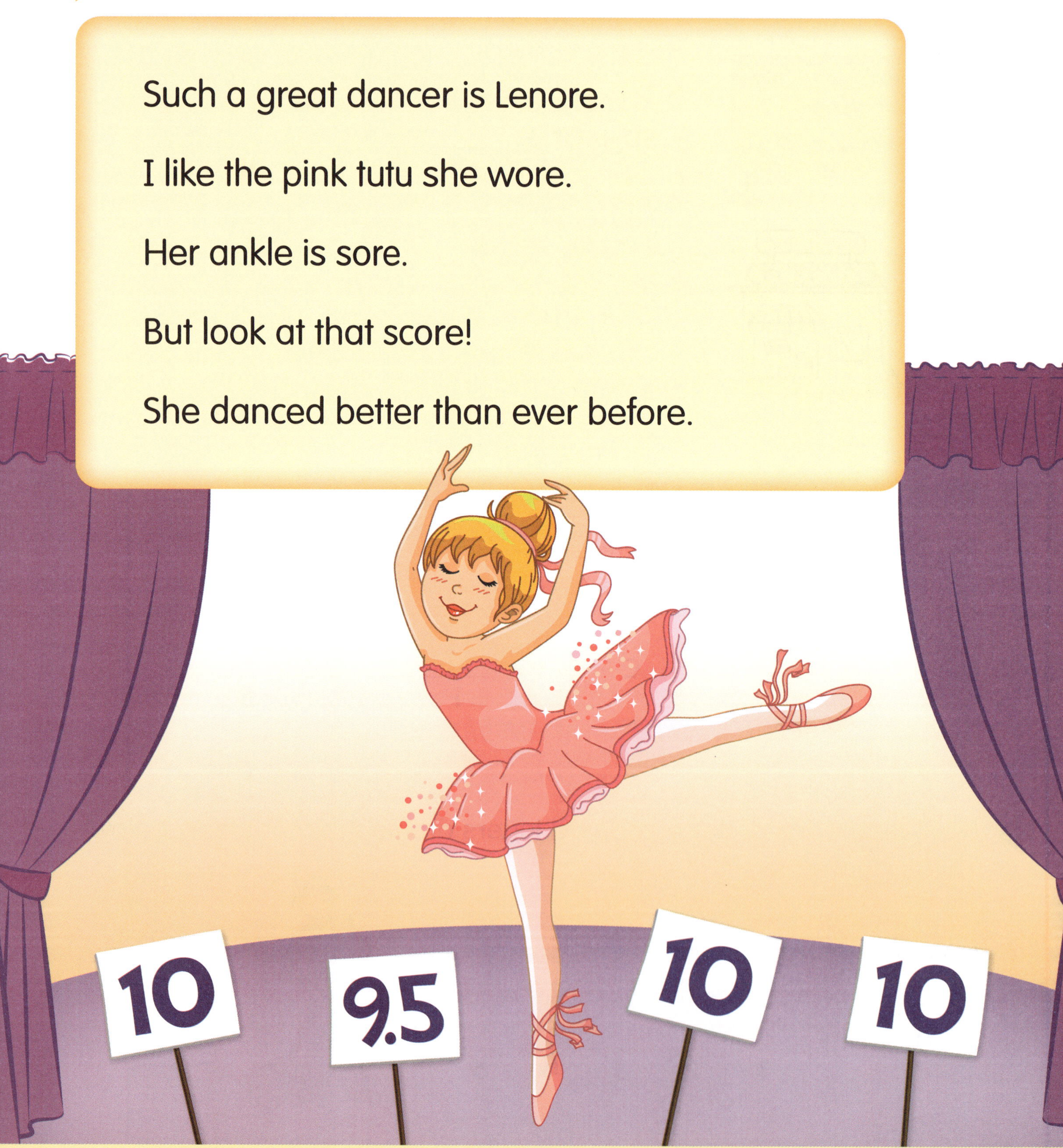

-ore at the Shore

Find the **-ore** words. Circle them.

Fill in the missing words.

1. Yesterday we went to the grocery __________.
2. But __________ we went shopping, we went to the beach.
3. I __________ shorts so I could get my feet wet.
4. I walked along the __________, picking up seashells.
5. I want to gather __________ shells for my collection.

-ead Word Family

Write the letters on the lines to make **-ead** words. Then sound out the words you wrote.

1  h + ead ___ ___ ___ ___ (2, 1)

2  br + ead ___ ___ ___ ___ ___ (3)

3  thr + ead ___ ___ ___ ___ ___ ___ (4)

4  spr + ead ___ ___ ___ ___ ___ ___ (5)

Now write each of the numbered letters on the matching lines below. Read the rhyme.

Go ___ ___ ___ ___ ___.
1 2 3 4 5

Bake some bread!

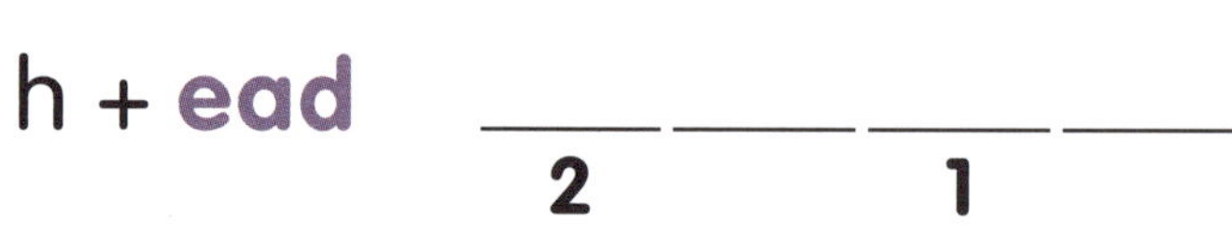

Bread and Thread

Read the poem. Underline the words in the **-ead** family.

There once was a baker named Fred.

He used to make cookies and bread.

But that was in June.

Now instead of a spoon,

He makes things with needle and thread.

Thread Clues

Read the clues along the thread.
Answer using words from the **-ead** family.

bread	thread	read
spread	dead	head

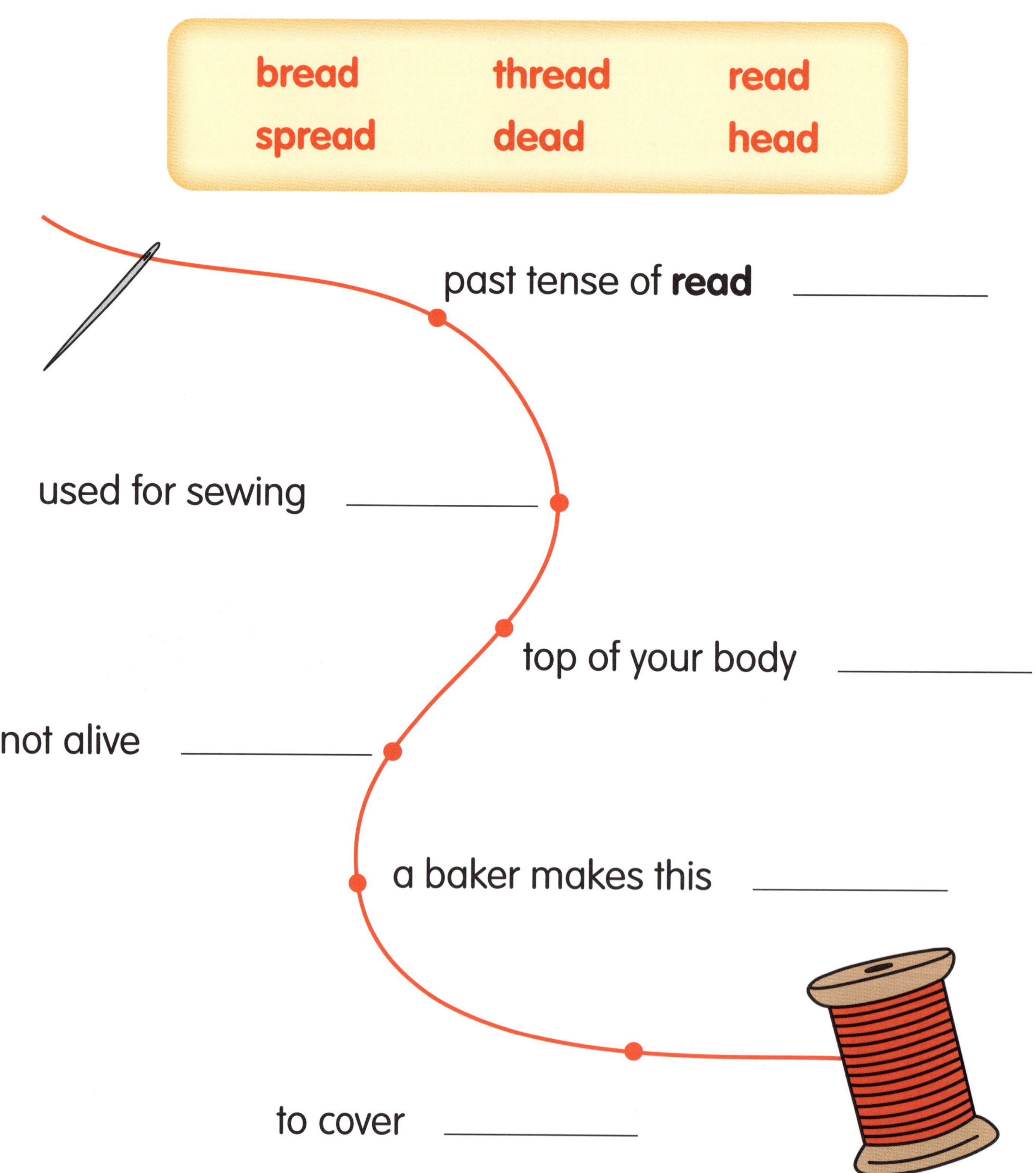

Write the letters on the lines to make **-ice** words. Then sound out the words you wrote.

1. 

m + ice ___ ___ ___ ___
(letter 3 numbered 4)

2. 

d + ice ___ ___ ___ ___
(letter 1 numbered 6, letter 2 numbered 3)

3. 

pr + ice ___ ___ ___ ___ ___
(letter 1 numbered 2, letter 2 numbered 7)

4. 

sl + ice ___ ___ ___ ___ ___
(letter 1 numbered 1, letter 5 numbered 5)

Now write each of the numbered letters on the matching lines below. Read the rhyme.

___ ___ ___ ___ ___ ___
1 2 3 4 5 6

___ ___ ___ ___ sure is nice!
7 3 4 5

Mice Ate My Rice

Read the poem. Underline the words in the **-ice** family.

I caught the mice eating my rice.

The rice had become cold as ice.

The mice did not care.

They're not a nice pair.

They've eaten my yummy rice twice.

Fun With Ice

Fill in the crossword puzzle using words with **-ice**.

Across

3. a type of grain

4. plural of **mouse**

6. two times

1

2

3 rice

4 5

6

$8.00

Down

1. a piece of pie

2. what something costs

5. frozen water

-ew Word Family

Write the letters on the lines to make **-ew** words.
Then sound out the words you wrote.

st + ew

____ ____ ____ ____
(blank 2: 5)

2 

ch + ew

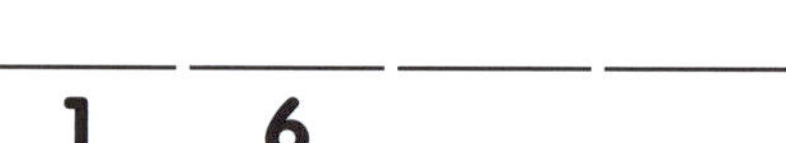

____ ____ ____ ____
(blank 1: 1, blank 2: 6)

3 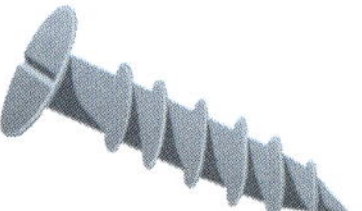

scr + ew ____ ____ ____ ____ ____
(blank 1: 7, blank 3: 2)

4 

dr + ew

____ ____ ____ ____
(blank 3: 3, blank 4: 4)

Now write each of the numbered letters on the matching lines below.
Read the rhyme.

The ____ ____ ____ ____ ____ ____ ____ ____ ____
(1 2 3 4 / 5 6 2 3 4)

a few ____ ____ ____ ____ ____ ____ in the trash.
(7 1 2 3 4 7)

Veggies for Stew

Read the poem. Underline the words in the **-ew** family.

I saw a few crows as they flew.

They wanted the veggies I grew.

The scarecrow is there

To give them a scare.

Since we need those veggies for stew!

Clue in the Stew

Read the clue in each bowl of stew. Write the word on each saucer.

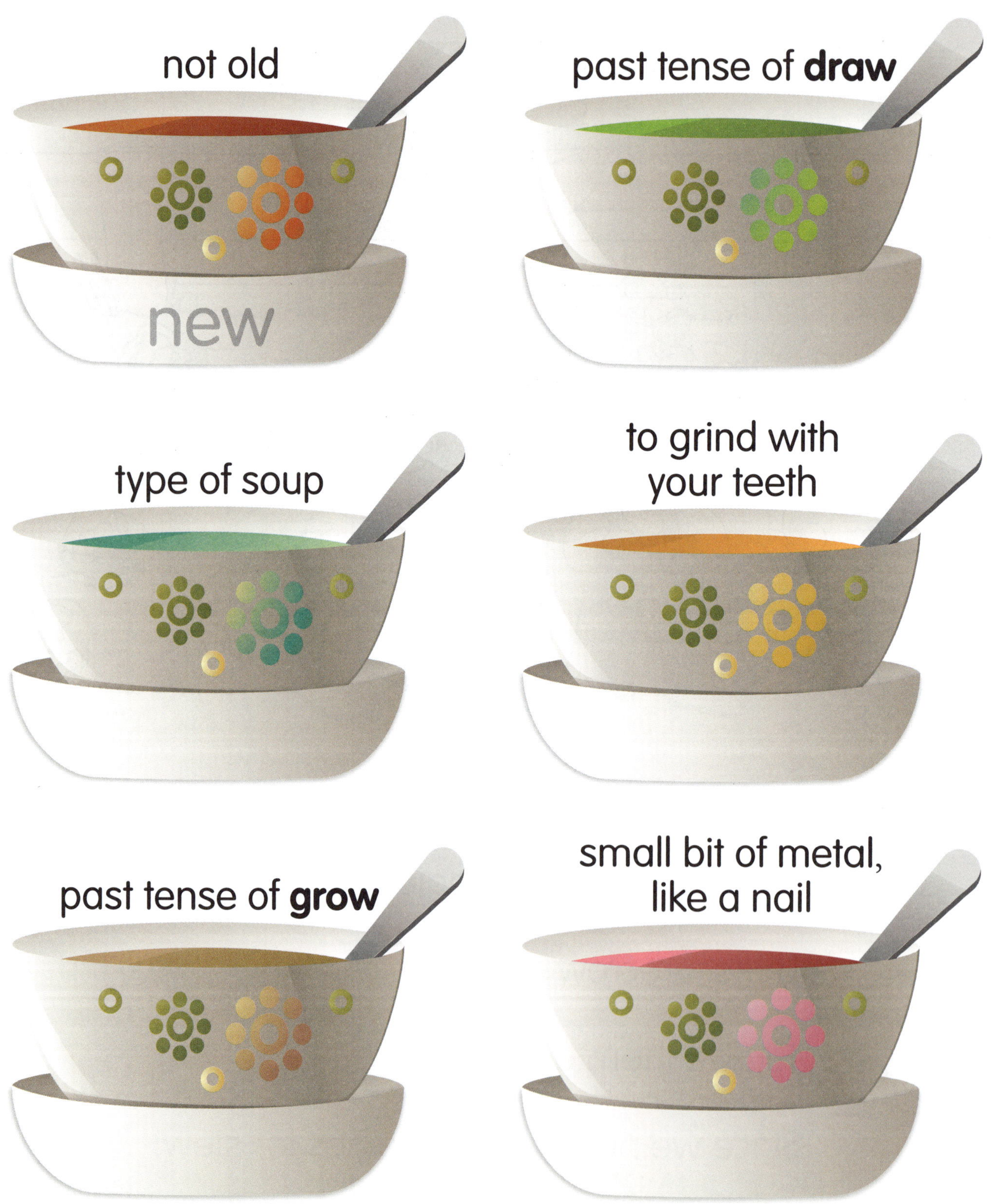

-ook Word Family

Write the letters on the lines to make **-ook** words.
Then sound out the words you wrote.

b + ook

4 3

2. 

c + ook ____ ____ ____ ____

2

3. 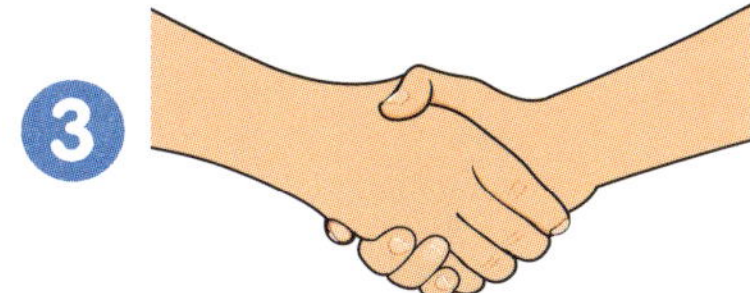

sh + ook ____ ____ ____ ____ ____

1

4. 

cr + ook ____ ____ ____ ____ ____

5

Now write each of the numbered letters on the matching lines below.
Read the rhyme.

I dropped my line and 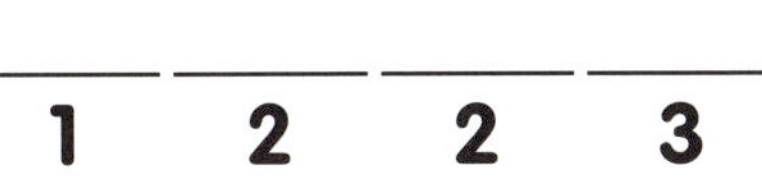

1 2 2 3

in the babbling 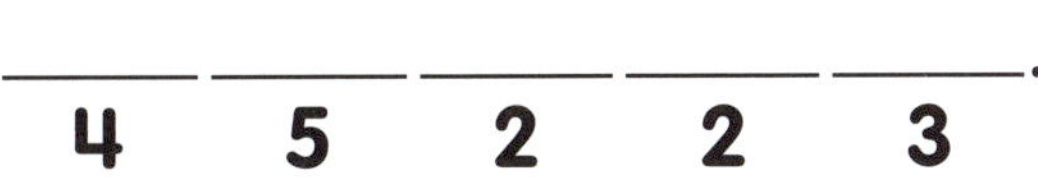.

4 5 2 2 3

The Pancake Crook

Read the story. Complete the story with words in the **-ook** family.

cook shook book took look mistook

This weekend, Dad ____________ us to Aunt Eva's house.

Aunt Eva is a good ____________. Her pancakes are great!

I wanted to make the pancakes, too. How hard could it be? I could ____________ in a ____________. I made the batter and poured it in the pan. Then I ____________ the pan, just as Aunt Eva does.

The pancake did not move. It was stuck! When I finally scraped it off, the stiff disc rolled onto the floor. Our playful pup ____________ it for a toy and ran off with it!

Nouns

A **noun** names a **person**, **place**, or **thing**.

person	place	thing
girl	school	car
boy	house	sun
friend	farm	flower
teacher	park	grass

The **girl** found her **car** near the **house**.

Nouns

Look at the picture. Use words from the box to finish the sentences.

hat friend kids gift

1. My ________________ had a party.

2. I got him a nice ________________.

3. I wore a funny ________________.

4. All the ________________ had fun.

Read the story. Circle the nouns in the story.

Play Ball!

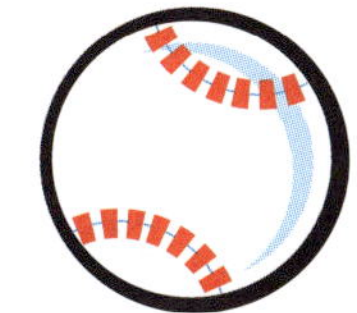

Three friends were at Lisa's house. They sat and sat. Then Lisa spotted a ball under the sofa. Henry went and got his bat. Lin got her mitt. They went to the park and played baseball.

Nouns

Find the correct noun to complete each sentence. Fill in the circle.

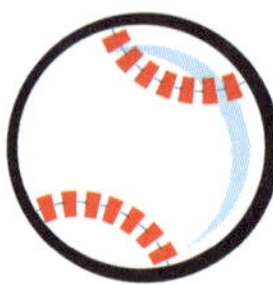

1. Lisa found a ________.

   ○ ball ○ bat

2. The ball was under the ________.

   ○ house ○ sofa

3. Henry had a ________.

   ○ mitt ○ bat

4. They played baseball in the ________.

   ○ park ○ house

Read the clue. Write the word on the lines.
Then figure out the secret message at the bottom.

1. People live here.

___ ___ ___ ___ ___
3 6 8 7 5

2. You hit a ball with this.

___ ___ ___
10 9 4

3. You catch a ball with this.

___ ___ ___ ___
1 2 4 4

4. Your pal is a ________.

___ ___ ___ ___ ___ ___
12 11 2 5 13 14

5. My best friend is a ________, not a boy.

___ ___ ___ ___
15 2 11 16

Secret Message

A noun names a person, place, or ___ ___ ___ ___ ___.
4 3 2 13 15

Nouns

Color all the nouns.

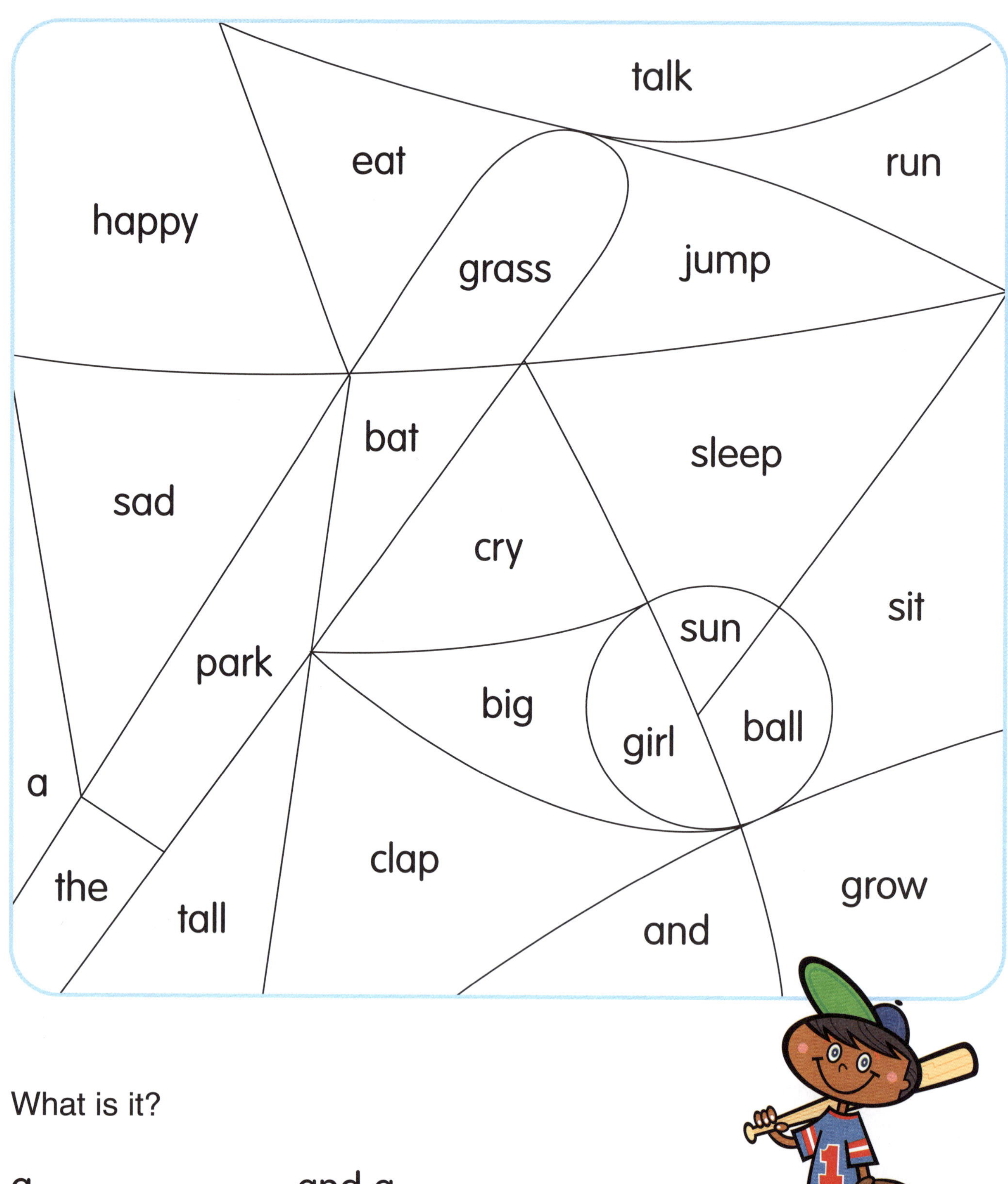

What is it?

a ______________ and a ______________

A **verb** tells **what is happening** or **what already happened**.

What is happening	What already happened
sit	sat
eat	ate
jump	jumped
sleep	slept
run	ran
talk	talked

Verbs

Look at the picture.
Use words from the box to finish the sentences.

jumped **kicked** **broke** **ate**

1. The goats ______________ the farmer's flowers.

2. When they saw him, they ______________ over the fence.

3. One goat ______________ the farmer's fence.

4. Another goat ______________ its heels with joy.

Read the story. Circle the verbs in the story.

What a mess! Toby escaped again.

He chased the neighbor's cat.

He spilled trash and

trampled the flowers.

He barked. He ran

here and there. Oh, Toby!

Verbs

Find the correct verb to complete each sentence. Fill in the circle.

1. Toby ________ the cat.

   ○ tripped ○ chased

2. Toby ________ the trash.

   ○ spilled ○ ate

3. Toby ________ the flowers.

   ○ trampled ○ picked

4. Toby ________ everywhere.

   ○ slept ○ ran

Verbs

Read the clue. Write the word on the lines.
Then figure out the secret message at the bottom.

1. to jump

___ ___ ___
1 5 2

2. to sleep

___ ___ ___
3 4 2

3. to ask for

___ ___ ___
6 8 7

4. to hit with the foot

___ ___ ___ ___
9 10 11 9

Secret Message

A verb tells what is

___ ___ ___ ___ ___ ___ ___ ___ ___.
1 4 2 2 8 3 10 3 7

Verbs

Color the verbs **green**.

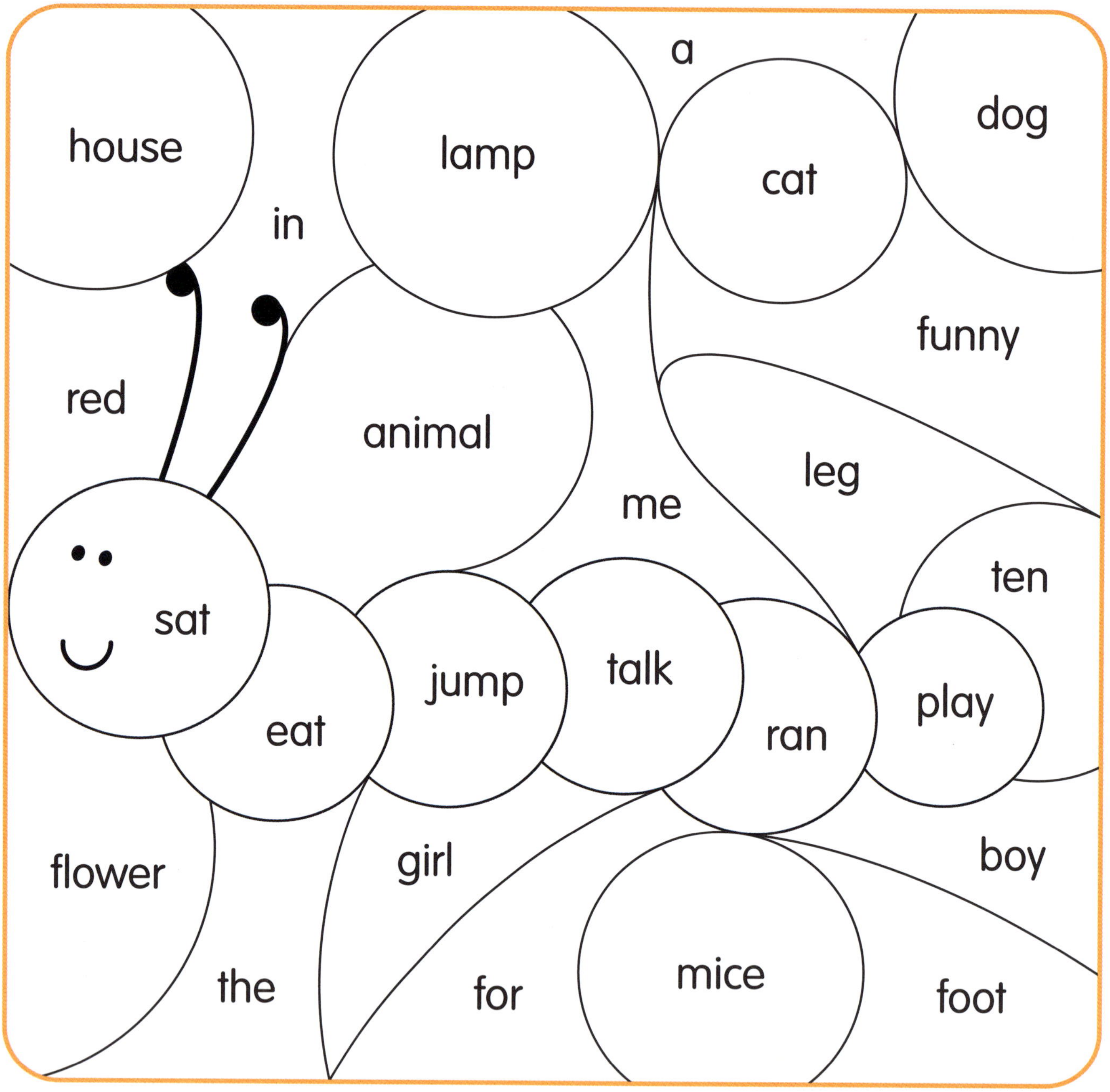

house in lamp a cat dog

red animal funny

me leg

sat eat jump talk ran play ten

flower girl boy

the for mice foot

fly swim crawl hop

This animal can ________________.

An **adjective** describes a noun.

The **big** watermelon
is very **sweet**.

The **hungry** goat
is behind a **strong wooden** fence.

Adjectives

Finish each sentence with an adjective from the word box.

sour juicy crunchy purple

1. I like green grapes, but

   ________________ grapes are my favorite.

2. I think yellow lemons are less

   ________________ than limes.

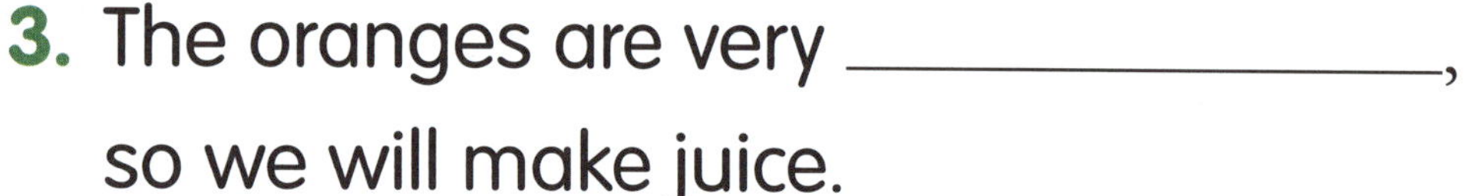

3. The oranges are very ________________,

   so we will make juice.

4. Our tree has lots of ________________ red apples.

Read the story. Circle the adjectives in the story.

We have a big tree in our yard.

The tree has many cherries.

Mom bakes yummy pies. Sometimes she makes creamy yogurt. Cherries also make a good snack for our lunches. I like cherries!

Adjectives

Find the best adjective to complete each sentence. Fill in the circle.

1. The family has a ________ tree.

   ○ big ○ small

2. Mom bakes ________ pies.

   ○ creamy ○ yummy

3. She makes yogurt that is ________.

   ○ creamy ○ sour

4. Cherries are a ________ snack for lunches.

   ○ big ○ good

Read the clue. Write the word on the lines.
Then figure out the secret message at the bottom.

1. A lemon tastes ________.

___ ___ ___ ___
4 7 2 5

2. A watermelon is not small; it is ________.

___ ___ ___
3 1 6

3. The pie is yummy! It is ________.

___ ___ ___ ___ ___ ___ ___ ___ ___
8 10 12 1 9 1 7 11 4

Secret Message

An adjective

___ ___ ___ ___ ___ ___ ___ ___ ___ a noun.
8 10 4 9 5 1 3 10 4

Adjectives

Read and draw. Then circle the adjectives.

green apples
in a big basket

a happy hen eating
juicy grapes

a worker carrying fresh
oranges on a sunny day

Pronouns

A **pronoun** can take the place of a noun.

That boy is Tom.

He is Tom.

Maya is smart.

She is smart.

My class is big.

It is big.

Look at the underlined words. Write each sentence again.
Use **He**, **She**, or **It**.

1. Henry is in my class. ________ is in my class.
2. Miss Reyes is our teacher. ________ is our teacher.
3. Our day starts at 8:15. ________ starts at 8:15.
4. School is fun! ________ is fun!

Pronouns

A plural pronoun can take the place of two or more nouns.

Milly and Molly are twins.

They are twins.

Beto, **Les**, **and I** are friends.

We are friends.

Look at the underlined words. Write each sentence again. Use **They** or **We**.

1. Ray and Sam each have a lunch.

   ___________ each have a lunch.

2. The kids are noisy.

   ___________ are noisy.

3. You, Celia, and I sit together.

   ___________ sit together.

4. You and I can share.

   ___________ can share.

Pronouns

Use **he** and **him** to talk about a **boy** or a **man**.

He is my brother. I like to play with **him**.

Use **she** and **her** to talk about a **girl** or a **woman**.

She is my sister. I like to play with **her**.

Look at the picture. Complete the sentences with **He**, **She**, **him**, or **her**.

1. ________ is sleeping.

   Don't wake ________.

2. ________ is Carla.

   Give ________ some milk.

3. ________ can sing.

   Just listen to ________!

4. ________ is having lunch.

   Ask ________ for a bite.

Pronouns

Use **I** and **me** to talk about **yourself**.

I walk to school.

Roy walks with **me**.

Read what Ruby and Sari are saying.
Complete each sentence by writing **I** or **me** on the line.

1. Sari, ________ am here!

   Okay. Wait for ________!

2. ________ have pizza for lunch.

   ________ do too!

3. Dad made it for ________.

   ________ love pizza.

4. Sit with ________ at lunch.

   ________ will!

Pronouns

Read the story. Circle the pronouns in the story.

I have lots of friends in school. First, there is Emily. I like her. We sit together at lunch. She is smart and she helps me to read. Sam is nice to me too. He plays baseball. He has played it since first grade. We play ball at recess with Ryan, Cory, and Sofia. They are good friends too.

Pronouns

Color the pronouns **red**. Color the word **and green**.

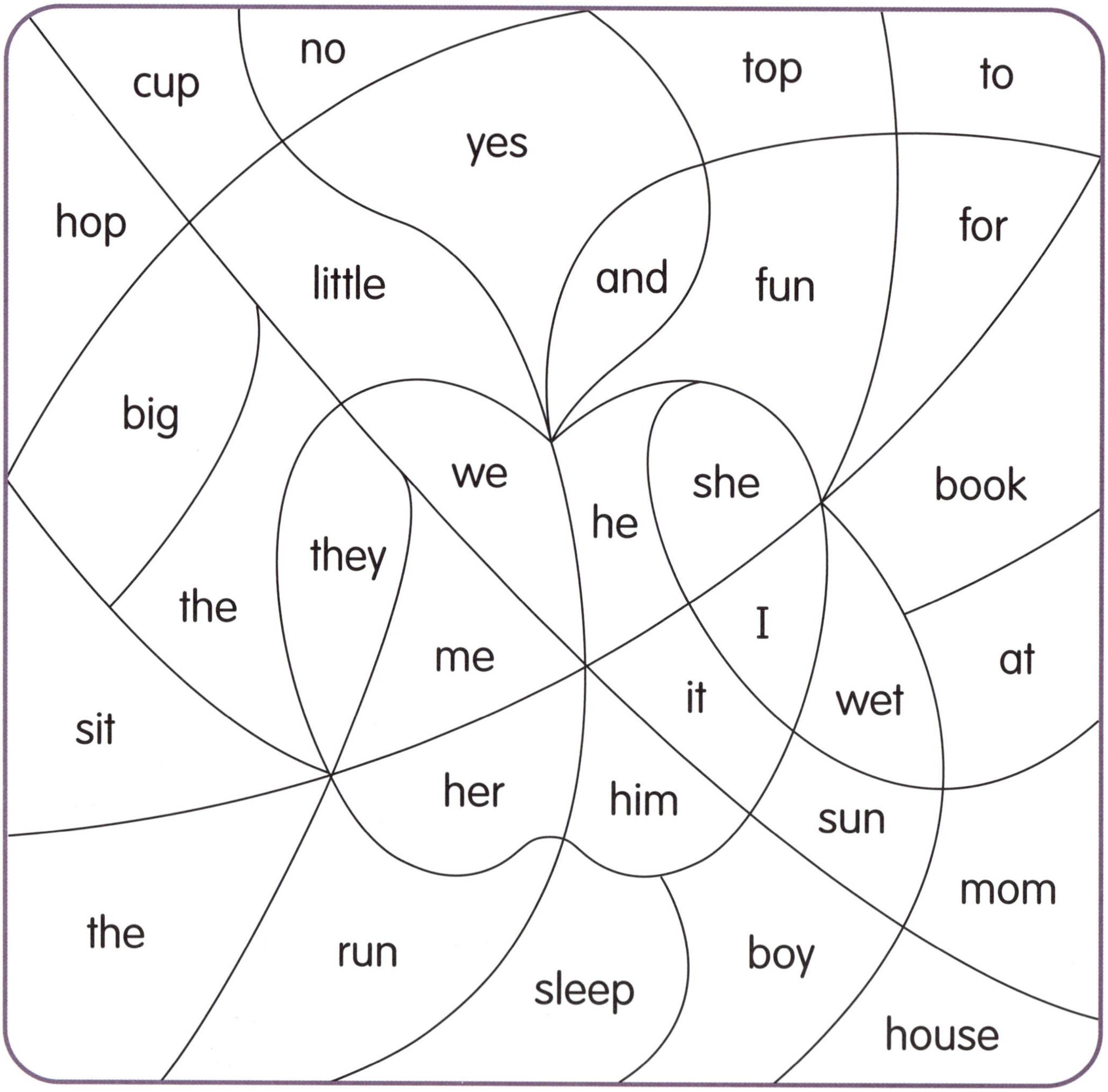

cup no yes top to
hop little and fun for
big we she book
the they he I at
sit me it wet
her him sun mom
the run sleep boy house

What is it?

It is an ______________.

Adverbs

An **adverb** tells **more about an action**.

How it happens	When it happens
loudly	often
well	later
softly	today
quietly	never

Adverbs

Look at the picture. Use words from the box to finish the sentences.

early **well** **soon** **brightly**

1. Mila woke up ________________ this morning.

2. The sun was shining ________________ through her window.

3. Mila's cat Sassy stretched ________________.

4. Mila and Sassy would play ________________.

Read the story. A few action words are underlined. Adverbs tell how or when. Circle the adverbs.

Mila and Sassy visit the park often. Today was a good day. A butterfly landed gently on Mila's hand. Can you believe it? It crawled to the tip of Mila's finger and softly fluttered its wings. Mila smiled and watched it closely.

Adverbs

Find the best adverb to complete each sentence.
Fill in the circle.

1. Mila and Sassy ________ visit the park.

   ○ often ○ never

2. A butterfly landed ________ on her hand.

   ○ suddenly ○ gently

3. It fluttered its wings ________.

   ○ softly ○ quickly

4. Mila watched the butterfly ________.

   ○ closely ○ oddly

Read the clue. Write the word on the lines.
Then figure out the secret message at the bottom.

1. not slowly

___ ___ ___ ___ ___ ___ ___
10 9 1 13 16 4 6

2. in a soft way

___ ___ ___ ___ ___ ___
8 7 3 5 4 6

3. with care

___ ___ ___ ___ ___ ___ ___ ___ ___
13 11 12 2 3 9 4 4 6

4. in a gentle way

___ ___ ___ ___ ___ ___
15 2 14 5 4 6

Secret Message

An adverb tells about an ___ ___ ___ ___ ___ ___.
11 13 5 1 7 14

In the Sandbox

Look at all the things in the sandbox. Each one is a **compound word** (a word made of two words put together). Use a word from each list to name the things in the sandbox.

✓ foot	flower
horse	pot
air	book
note	shoe
tea	plane
sun	✓ ball

football ____________________

____

____

____

____

____

Rainy Day Compounds

Use words from both clouds to make **compound words**. Label the picture.

Complete each compound word.

__________bow

__________drops

__________fall

__________coat

Rhyme Time

Here are some fun riddles to solve.
The answer will be two words that rhyme.

What do you call
a happy father?

glad dad

Match the riddle with the answer.

baked goodie that's not real	**fat cat**
watery aircraft	**mouse house**
plump feline	**best nest**
rodent home	**fake cake**
great birdie home	**wet jet**

Find the Rhymes

Find the words that rhyme.
Write them on the lines.

dark	big	rest
run	bee	skunk
beef	bean	ball

tree ______	sun ______	bark ______
trunk ______	twig ______	nest ______
leaf ______	fall ______	green ______

Prefix re-

Word parts can be added to base words to make new words.

A **prefix** can be added to the beginning of a base word to make a new word.

The prefix **re-** means "**to do again**."

re + use = reuse Please reuse this paper.

Make four new words with **re-**.

________________ ________________

________________ ________________

Now write a sentence using one or more of the words.

____

____

Prefixes mis- and dis-

The prefixes **mis-** and **dis-** both mean "**not**."

Answer these clues. Use the word box to help you.

disobey **misspell** **dishonest** **misdial** **disbelieve**

to write a word wrong __ __(2) __ __ __ __ __ __

to get a wrong number __(1) __ __ __ __ __(7) __

to not believe __ __ __ __ __(5) __ __ __ __(8) __

not honest __ __ __ __(6) __ __ __ __ __

to not obey __ __ __(3) __ __(4) __ __

Why is the girl angry?

Because her dog

__ __ __ __ __ __ __ __ __ __ .
1 2 3 4 5 6 7 8 5 3

Prefix pre-

The prefix **pre-** means "**before.**"

Draw a line to match.

to pay before	**preview**
to take a peek	**preheat**
to clean something	**preschool**
to warm up the oven	**prepay**
the time before kindergarten	**prewash**

Suffixes -er and -ist

Each word in the word box has the suffix **-er** or **-ist**, which mean "**one who does.**" Find the words in the puzzle. Circle them.

baker	writer	teacher
artist	tourist	driver
guitarist		

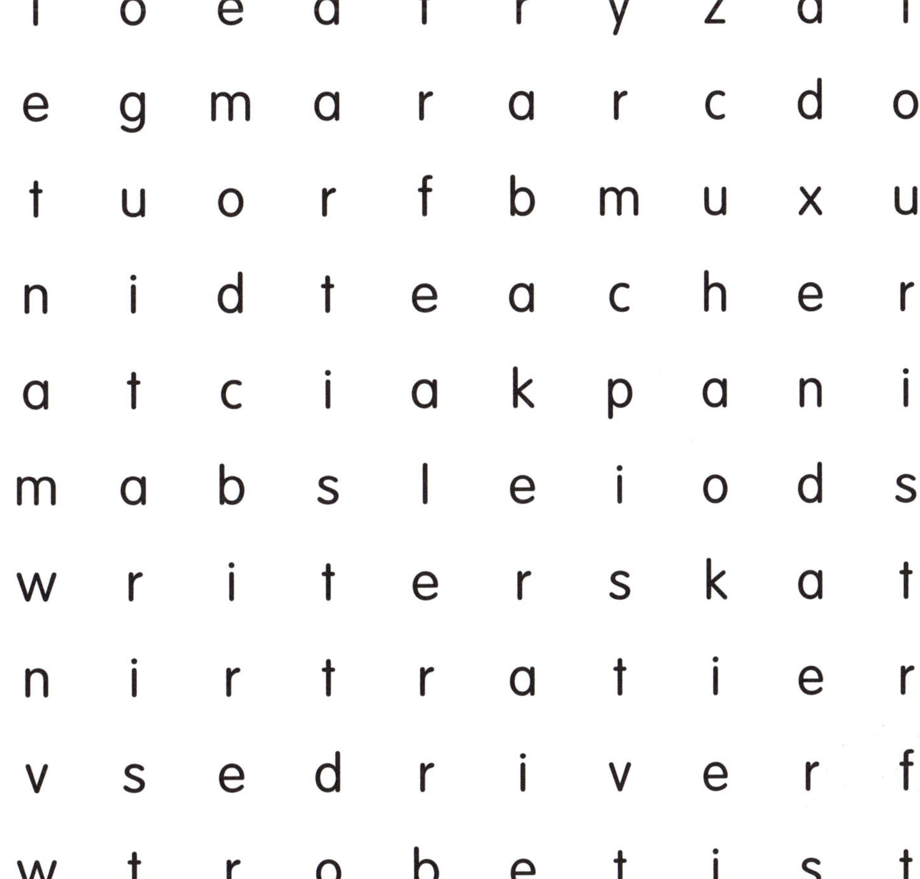

l	o	e	d	t	r	y	z	a	t
e	g	m	a	r	a	r	c	d	o
t	u	o	r	f	b	m	u	x	u
n	i	d	t	e	a	c	h	e	r
a	t	c	i	a	k	p	a	n	i
m	a	b	s	l	e	i	o	d	s
w	r	i	t	e	r	s	k	a	t
n	i	r	t	r	a	t	i	e	r
v	s	e	d	r	i	v	e	r	f
w	t	r	o	b	e	t	i	s	t

Suffixes -ful and -less

Fill in each column with words that end with **-ful** or **-less**. Use words from the word box.

thought	spoon	joy	fear
care	color	hand	help

Suffixes -able and -ment

The suffix **-able** means "**can be done.**"

The suffix **-ment** means "**the result of doing something.**"

Answer these clues. Use the word box to help you.

movement	washable	agreement	walkable

the result of agreeing ___ ___ ___ ___ ___ ___ ___ ___ ___
(2 under the 3rd blank)

can be washed ___ ___ ___ ___ ___ ___ ___ ___
(4 under the 2nd blank; 1 under the 6th blank)

can be walked ___ ___ ___ ___ ___ ___ ___ ___
(5 under the 4th blank; 6 under the 7th blank)

the result of moving ___ ___ ___ ___ ___ ___ ___ ___
(3 under the 6th blank)

Why did the clay pot break?

It was

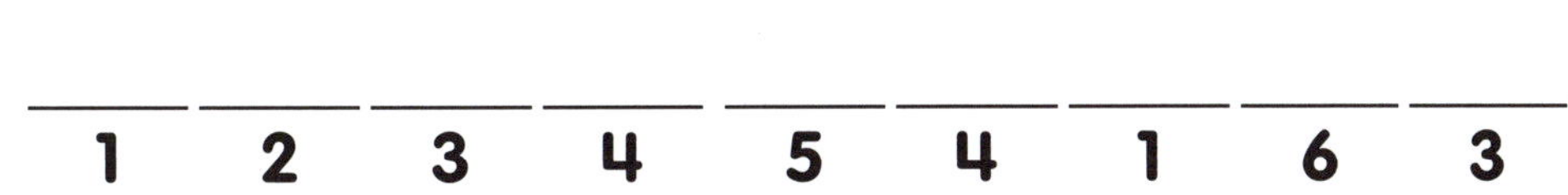

Beginning and End

Read each word in the box. Circle each prefix or suffix. Use the words to complete the puzzle.

comfortable	batter
payment	writer
mistreat	review
reusable	

Down

1. cozy
3. to see again
5. he hits the baseball

Across

2. to treat badly
4. can use again
6. money for something
7. one who writes

Unscramble the letters in the green boxes to answer the clue:

to tell again ___ ___ ___ ___ ___ ___

Synonym Verbs and Nouns

A **synonym** is a word that means **almost the same**.
Write the two synonyms under each picture.

Synonym Buns

A synonym is a word that means almost the same.
Read the word in the bottom part of the cinnamon bun.
Write a synonym on the icing.

yummy thin buddy nap huge auto

Synonym Crossword

Write a word that means almost the same (synonym). Use the word box to help you.

hop	angry	look	road
grab	small	false	damp

1. untrue
4. take
6. see
8. moist

Down

2. mad
3. little
5. street
7. jump

Unscramble the letters in the green boxes to answer the clue:

A synonym means the ___ ___ ___ ___.

Antonym Match

Lori and May are like night and day.
If Lori says it's hot, May says it's cold.
Draw a line from Lori's words to May's opposite words (**antonyms**).

big	thin
thick	close
wet	little
open	hard
soft	sour
sweet	dry

Antonym Crossword

Write the opposite (antonym) of the word given.
Use the word box to help you.

Down

1. out
2. slow
3. white
5. sad

Across

4. short
6. cold
7. dirty
8. bottom
9. no

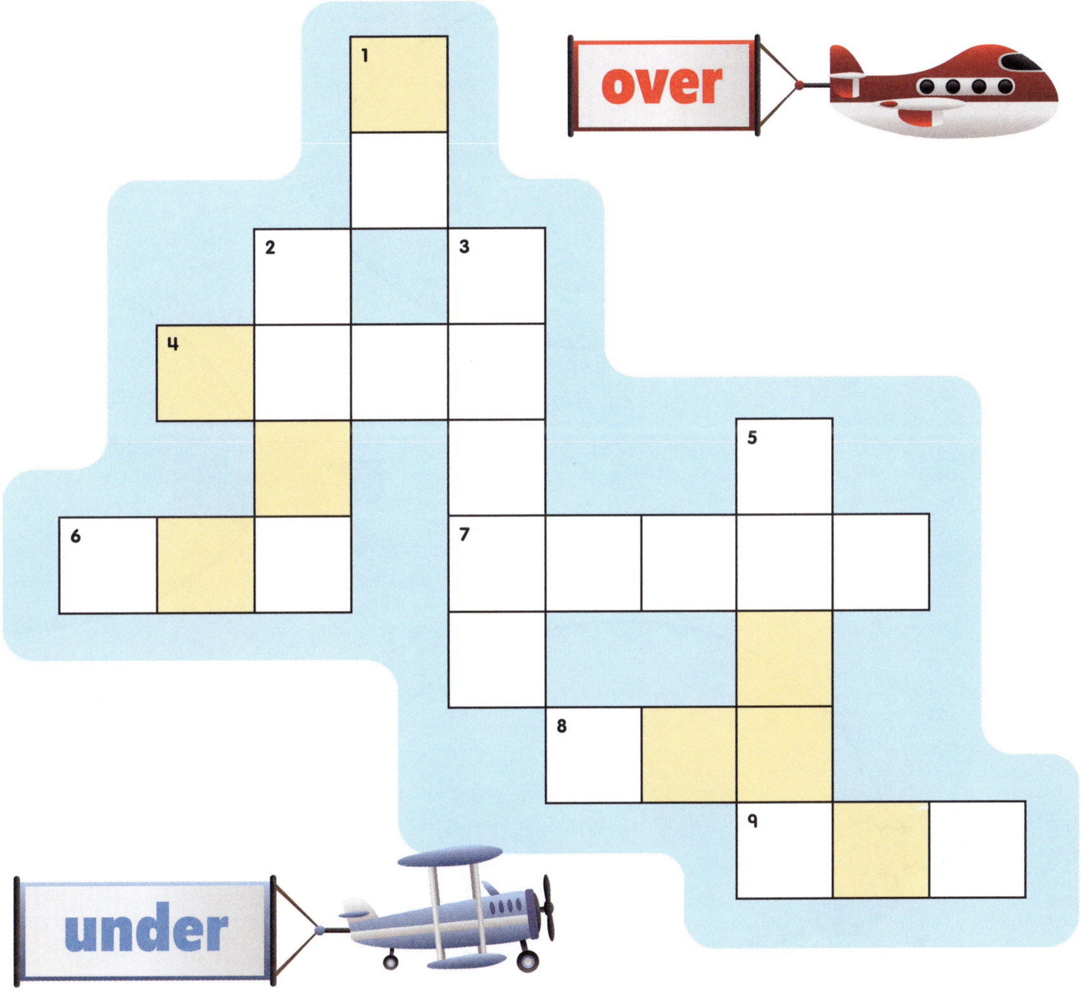

over

under

Unscramble the letters in the yellow boxes to answer the clue:

An antonym means the ____ ____ ____ ____ ____ ____ ____ ____.

Ant, Ant, Antonym

These ants are carrying antonyms.
Write pairs of antonyms on the leaves.
Use words from the word box.

asleep	good	back	bad	front	awake

asleep

Some words sound alike, but they have different meanings.

A **fly can fly** into a **can**.

Look at the clues. Write the word from the word box that goes with both clues.

sink **wave** **park** **trip** **bat** **saw**

say hello	sea moves	________
stop a car	place with trees	________
baseball	flying mammal	________
fall down	travel	________
past of **see**	tool to cut with	________
wash your hands	fall below water	________

Homophone Crossword

Some words sound alike, but they have different meanings and spellings.

It is fun to **be** a **bee**.

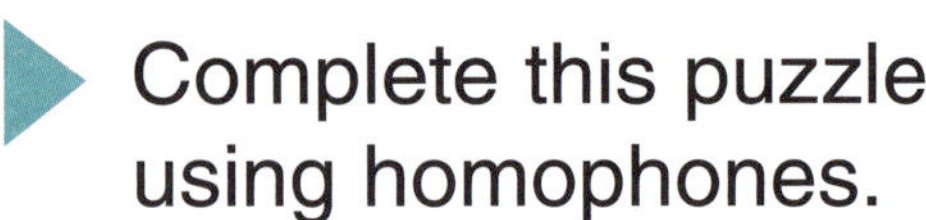

Complete this puzzle using homophones.

Across

2. plain
4. tale
5. see
7. right
9. too
11. knew

Down

1. flour
2. pane
3. knows
6. aunt
8. rose
10. won

Telephone Homophones

Find the homophones in the telephone. Circle them.
Use the word boxes to help you.

BEAT BEET

MAIN MANE

MAIL MALE

SO SEW

PIECE PEACE

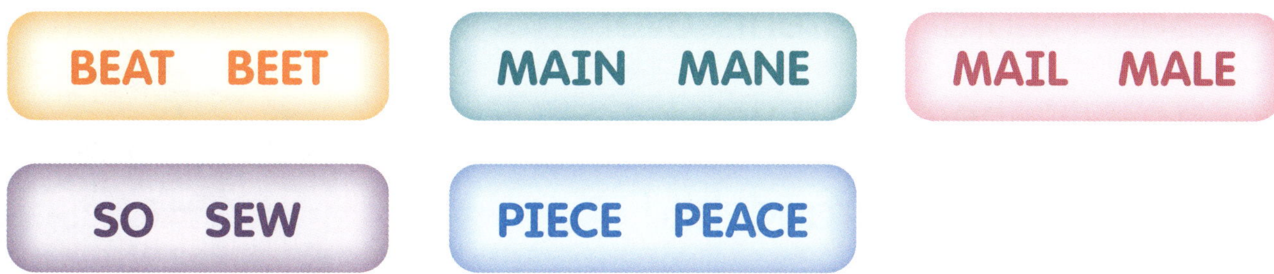

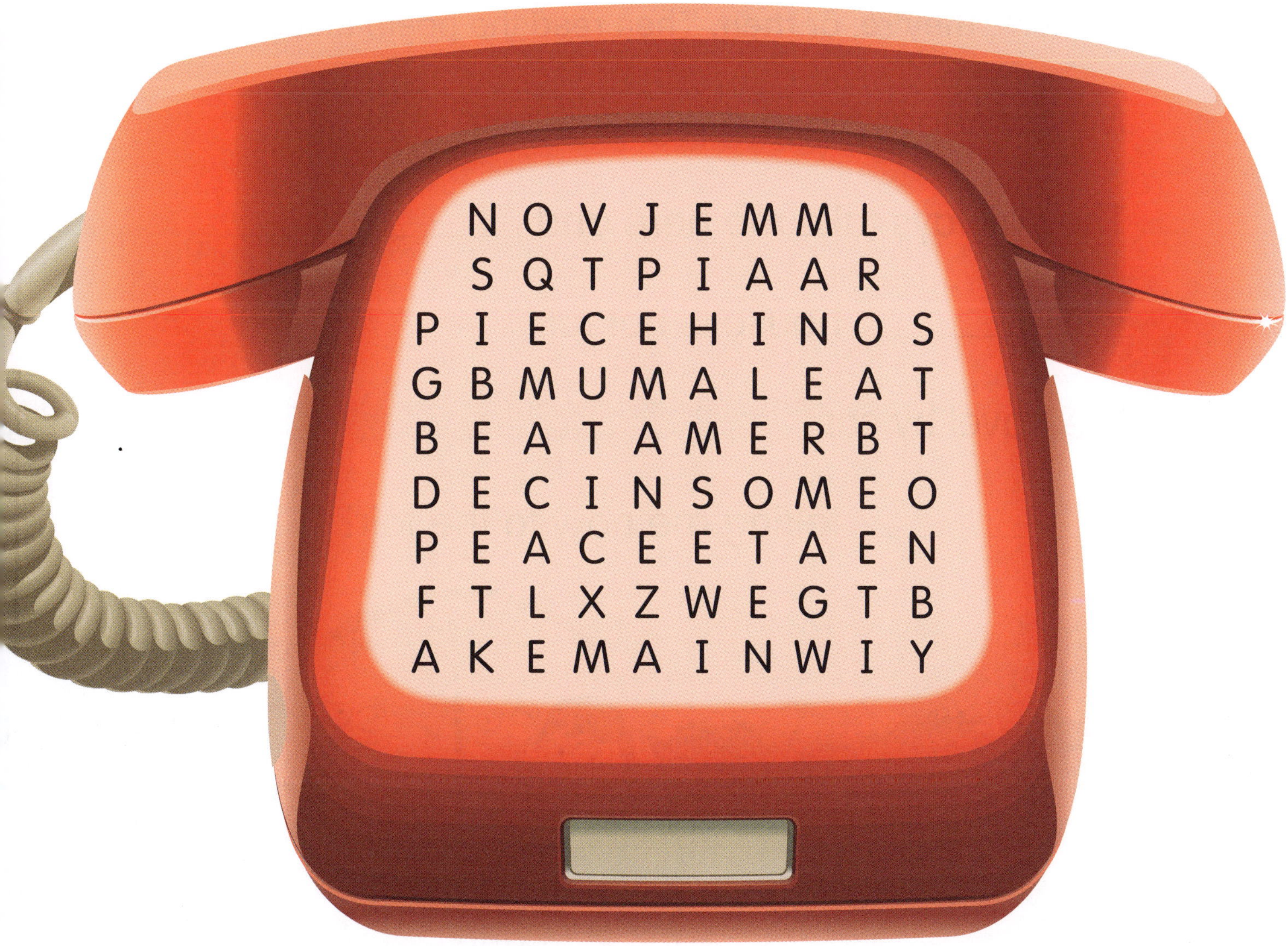

N O V J E M M L
S Q T P I A A R
P I E C E H I N O S
G B M U M A L E A T
B E A T A M E R B T
D E C I N S O M E O
P E A C E E T A E N
F T L X Z W E G T B
A K E M A I N W I Y

There, They're, Their

There, **they're**, and **their** are **homophones**.

See my grandparents over **there**?

They're here for a week.

I'm **their** only grandchild.

Write **there**, **they're**, or **their**. Then read the poem aloud.

My grandparents are a grand pair.

They always take me here and ____________.

____________ house is not far.

We travel by car.

____________ taking me now to the fair!

It's means "**it is**."

It is raining. **It's** raining.

Its shows **possession**.

The tree lost **its** leaves.

Write **it's** or **its**.
Then read the poem aloud.

_____________ raining.
_____________ pouring.
_____________ time to go exploring.

A bird is in _____________ nest
And it will do _____________ best
To keep _____________ babies dry
This wet and windy morning.

You're, Your

You're means "**you are**."

You are my best friend.

You're my best friend.

Your shows **possession**.

Here is **your** gift.

Write **you're** or **your**.
Then sing the song to the tune of "Happy Birthday."

It's ____________ big day. Hooray!

____________ a good friend, I say.

All ____________ pals are together.

And ____________ going to play!

Plural -s

A singular noun names one. A plural noun names more than one. Add **-s** to most nouns to make them plural.

  apple**s**

 orange**s**

Carmen is making something yummy. Answer the clues to find out what it is.

grapes **bananas** **almonds** **plums**

These are sweet and sour __ __ __ __ __ (2nd letter numbered 3)

These come in green bunches __ __ __ __ __ __ (6th letter numbered 1)

Monkeys love these __ __ __ __ __ __ __ (2nd letter numbered 2)

These are a kind of nut __ __ __ __ __ __ __ (6th letter numbered 4)

What is Carmen making?

Fruit __ __ __ __ __
1 2 3 2 4

Bunches of Peaches

Add **-s** to most nouns to make them plural.
Add **-es** to nouns that end in **ch**, **sh**, **s**, or **x**.

▶ Read the rhyme.
Underline the plural nouns.
Write them in the correct box.

Among green branches
the farmer reaches
for ripe and yellow
fuzzy peaches.

Slowly he fills
boxes and sacks
And saves bunches
for lunches and snacks.

The fruit is perfect
for special peach dishes
like cobblers and pies.
Oh! So delicious!

Plurals with -s

Plurals with -es

Babies and Butterflies

Some nouns end in a consonant **+ y**.
Change the **y** to **i** and add **-es** to make the plural.

sky ⟶ skies

▶ Answer the clues. Use the word box to help you.

lady	butterfly	puppy	kitty	baby

cats ___ ___ ___ ___ ___ ___ ___
(4 under 1st blank)

young dogs ___ ___ ___ ___ ___ ___ ___
(1 under 3rd blank)

young people ___ ___ ___ ___ ___ ___

_____ and gentlemen ___ ___ ___ ___ ___ ___
(2 under 2nd blank)

insects ___ ___ ___ ___ ___ ___ ___ ___ ___ ___ ___
(3 under 6th blank)

▶ Where can you find all these?

in a ___ ___ ___ ___
1 2 3 4

Loaves and Leaves

Some nouns end in **f** or **fe**. Change the **f** to **v** and add **-es**.

wolf wolves

Sometimes you just add **-s**, though.

giraffe giraffes

Answer the clues. Use the word box to help you.

leaf	loaf	calf	shelf	wolf

baby cows ___ ___ ___ ___ ___ ___ (6)

these grow on trees ___ ___ ___ ___ ___ ___ (5)

books go here ___ ___ ___ ___ ___ ___ ___ (1, 3)

these animals howl ___ ___ ___ ___ ___ ___ (4)

_____ of bread ___ ___ ___ ___ ___ ___ (2)

When you cut a loaf of bread in half,

you get two ___ ___ ___ ___ ___ ___ .
1 2 3 4 5 6

Men, Women, and Children

Some plural nouns have special spellings. Complete the puzzle using special plurals.

Across

4. mouse
5. tooth
6. man

Down

1. child
2. foot
3. woman

Unscramble the letters in the green boxes to answer the clue:

Men, women, and children are all

p___ ___p___ ___.

One Fish, Two Fish

Some special nouns are spelled the same in both singular and plural.

Read the poem. Decide if the underlined noun is singular or plural. If it is **singular**, circle it in **green**. If it is **plural**, circle it in **blue**.

A tired sheep,
Fast asleep,
Saw three red fish.
Swish, swish, swish.
Two big moose
Were drinking juice.
And a baby deer
Was standing near.

Plural Review

Complete the puzzle using plurals.

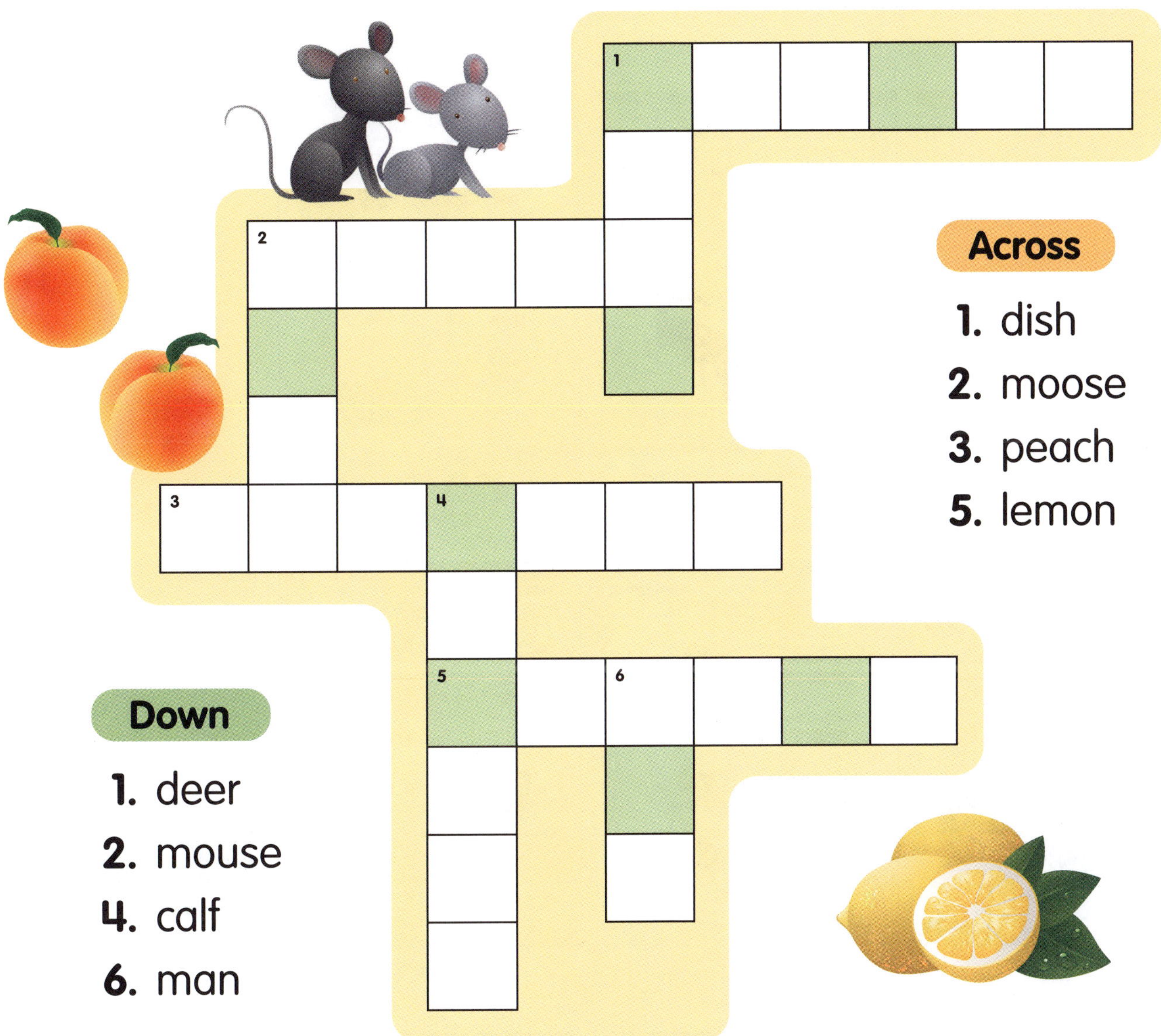

Across

1. dish
2. moose
3. peach
5. lemon

Down

1. deer
2. mouse
4. calf
6. man

Unscramble the letters in the green boxes to answer the clue:

plural of **child** ___ ___ ___ ___ ___ ___ ___ ___

Answer Key

Please take time to go over the work your child has completed. Ask your child to explain what he or she has done. Praise both success and effort. If mistakes have been made, explain what the answer should have been and how to find it. Let your child know that mistakes are a part of learning. The time you spend with your child helps let him or her know you feel learning is important.

Page 2

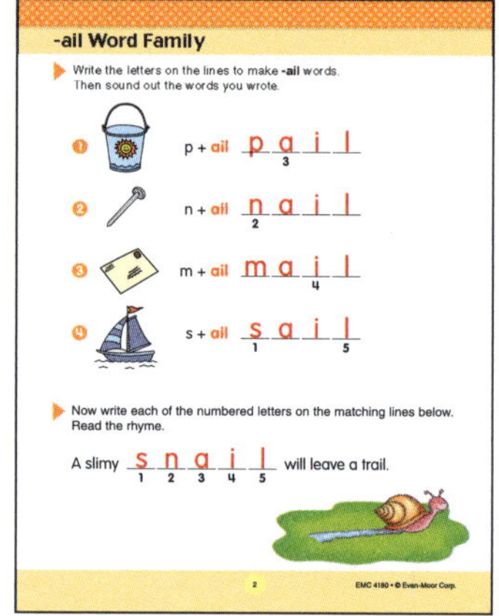

Page 3

Page 4

Page 5

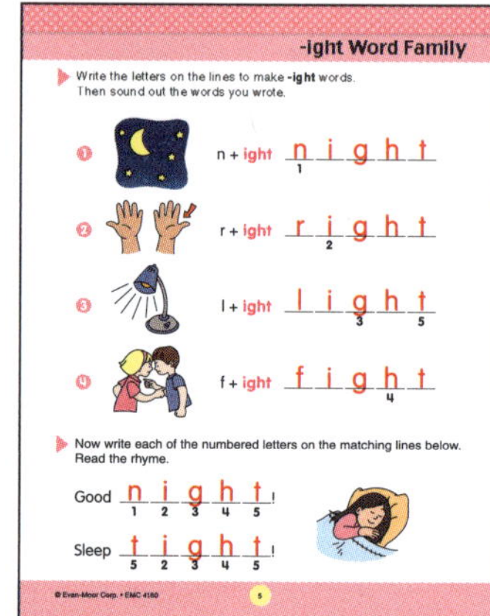

Page 6

Page 7

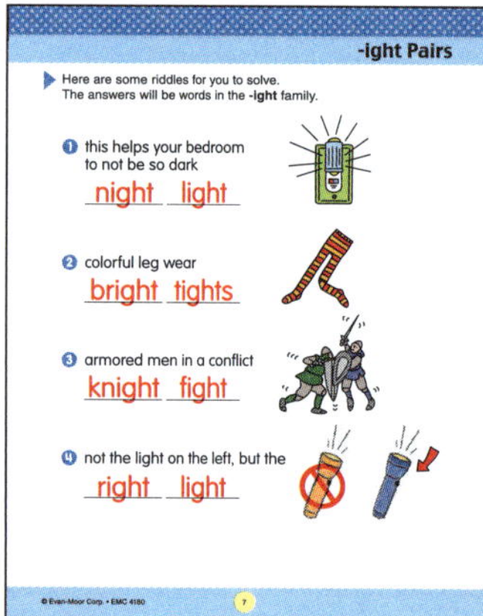

Page 8

Page 9

Page 10

Page 11

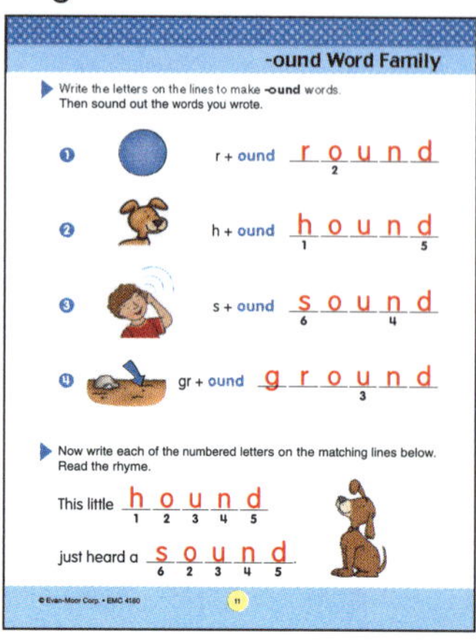

Page 12

Page 13

Page 14

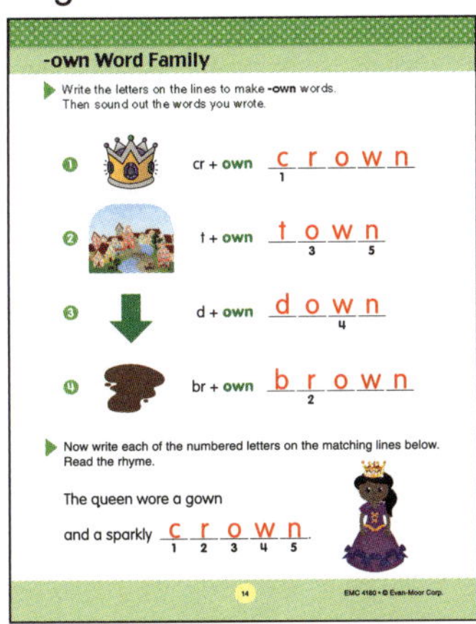

Page 15

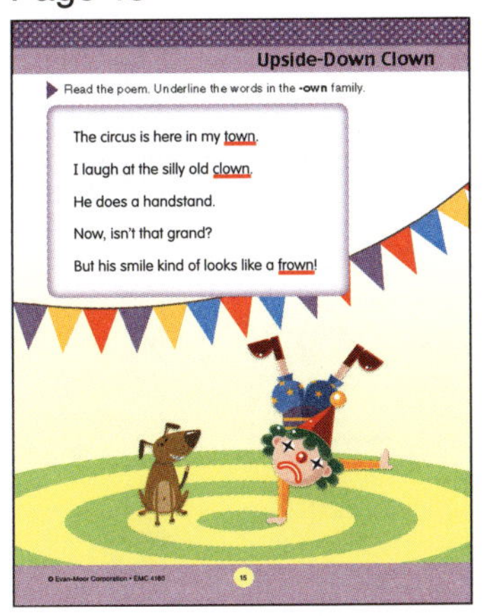

Page 16

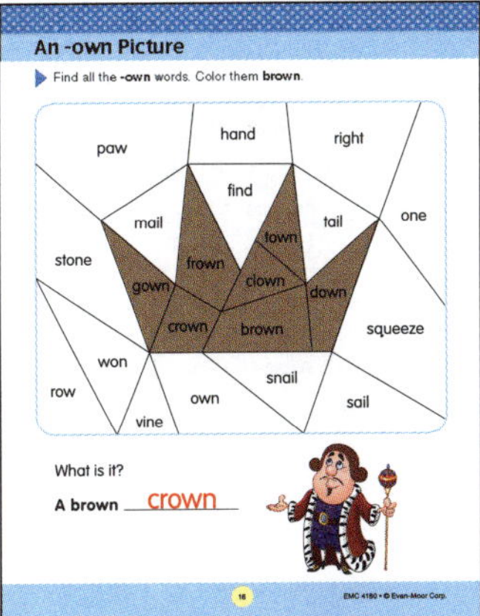

Page 17

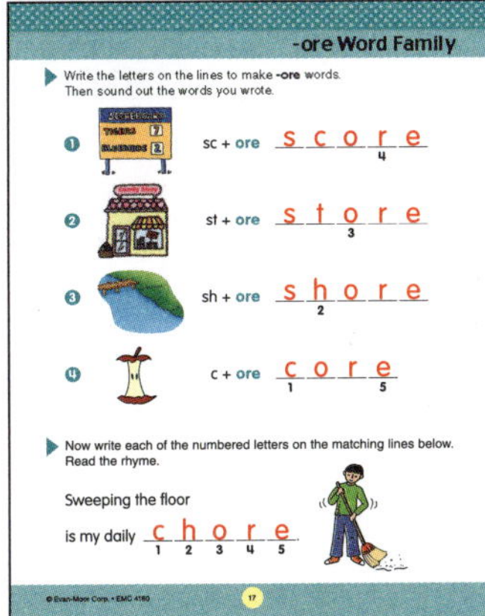

Page 18

Page 19

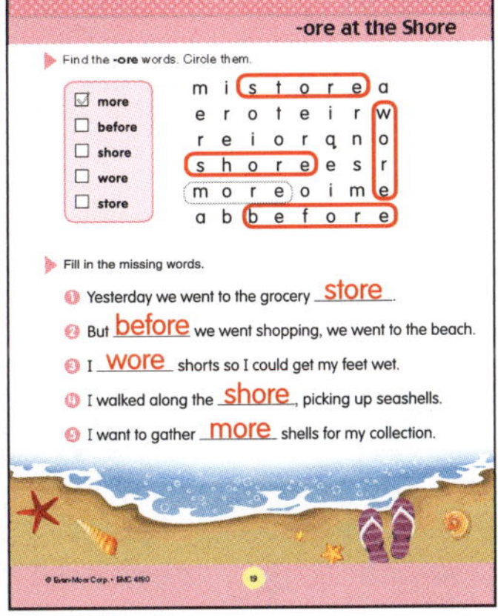

Page 20

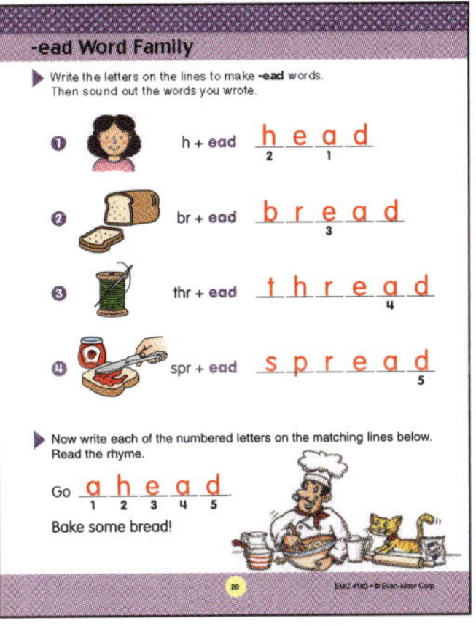

Page 21

Page 22

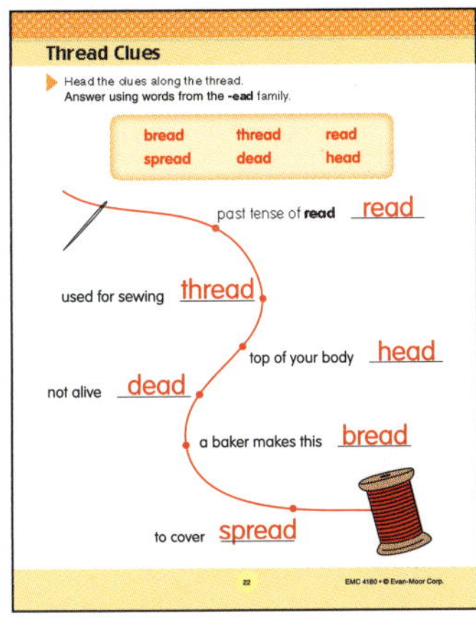

Page 23

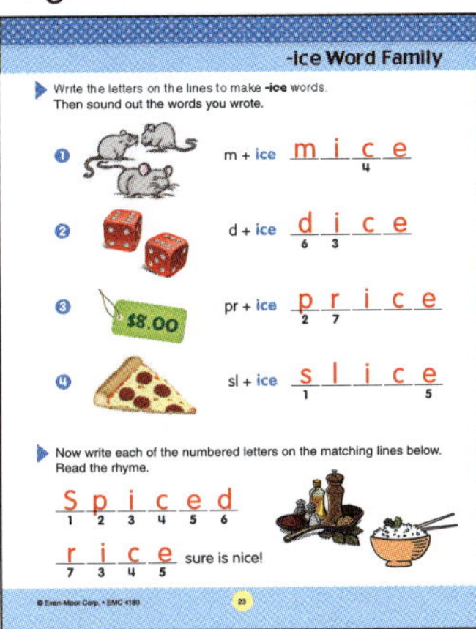

Page 24

Page 25

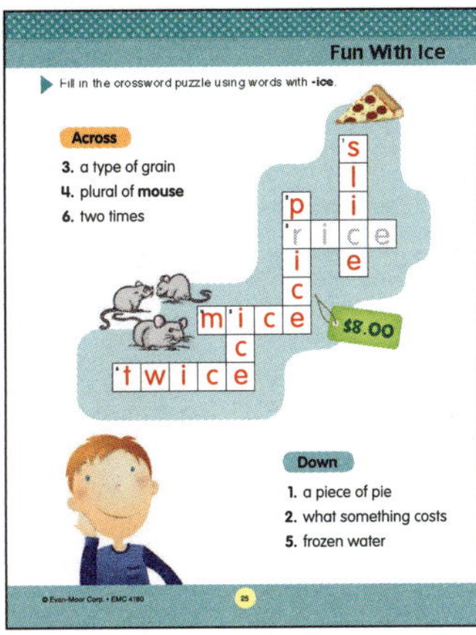

Page 26

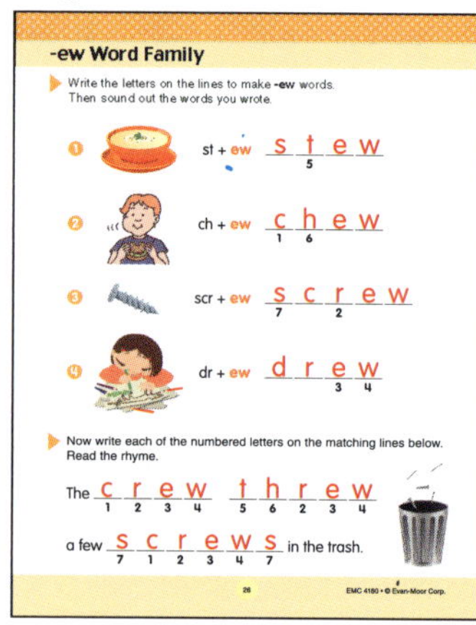

-ew Word Family

Write the letters on the lines to make **-ew** words. Then sound out the words you wrote.

1. st + ew s t e w
2. ch + ew c h e w
3. scr + ew s c r e w
4. dr + ew d r e w

Now write each of the numbered letters on the matching lines below. Read the rhyme.

The c r e w t h r e w a few s c r e w s in the trash.

Page 27

Veggies for Stew

Read the poem. Underline the words in the **-ew** family.

I saw a few crows as they flew.
They wanted the veggies I grew.
The scarecrow is there
To give them a scare.
Since we need those veggies for stew!

Page 28

Clue in the Stew

Read the clue in each bowl of stew. Write the word on each saucer.

- not old — new
- past tense of **draw** — drew
- type of soup — stew
- to grind with your teeth — chew
- past tense of **grow** — grew
- small bit of metal, like a nail — screw

Page 29

-ook Word Family

Write the letters on the lines to make **-ook** words. Then sound out the words you wrote.

1. b + ook b o o k
2. c + ook c o o k
3. sh + ook s h o o k
4. cr + ook c r o o k

Now write each of the numbered letters on the matching lines below. Read the rhyme.

I dropped my line and h o o k in the babbling b r o o k.

Page 30

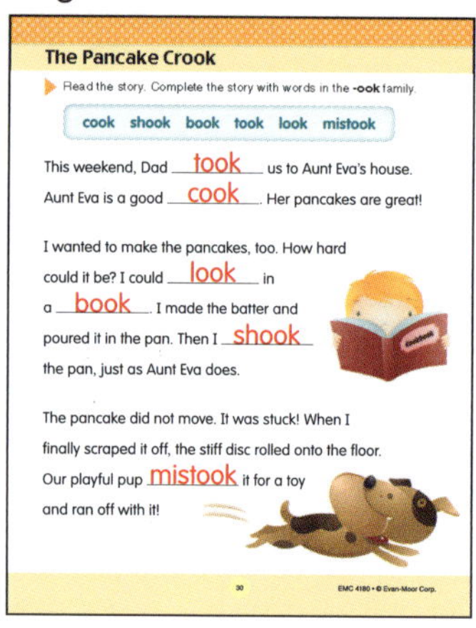

The Pancake Crook

Read the story. Complete the story with words in the **-ook** family.

cook shook book took look mistook

This weekend, Dad took us to Aunt Eva's house. Aunt Eva is a good cook. Her pancakes are great!

I wanted to make the pancakes, too. How hard could it be? I could look in a book. I made the batter and poured it in the pan. Then I shook the pan, just as Aunt Eva does.

The pancake did not move. It was stuck! When I finally scraped it off, the stiff disc rolled onto the floor. Our playful pup mistook it for a toy and ran off with it!

Page 32

Nouns

Look at the picture. Use words from the box to finish the sentences.

hat friend kids gift

1. My friend had a party.
2. I got him a nice gift.
3. I wore a funny hat.
4. All the kids had fun.

Page 33

Nouns

Read the story. Circle the nouns in the story.

Play Ball!

Three friends were at Lisa's house. They sat and sat. Then Lisa spotted a ball under the sofa. Henry went and got his bat. Lin got her mitt. They went to the park and played baseball.

Page 34

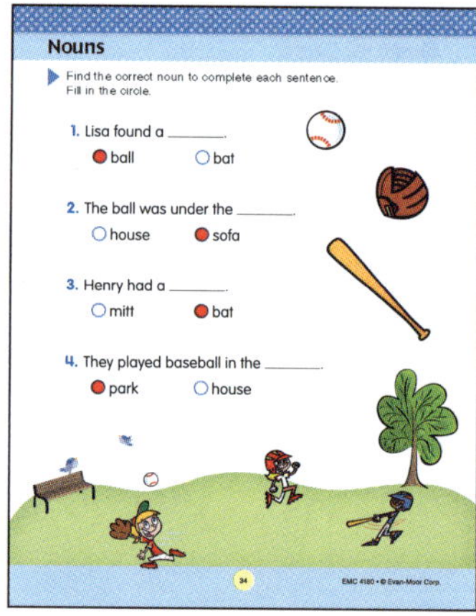

Nouns

Find the correct noun to complete each sentence. Fill in the circle.

1. Lisa found a ______. ● ball ○ bat
2. The ball was under the ______. ○ house ● sofa
3. Henry had a ______. ○ mitt ● bat
4. They played baseball in the ______. ● park ○ house

Page 35

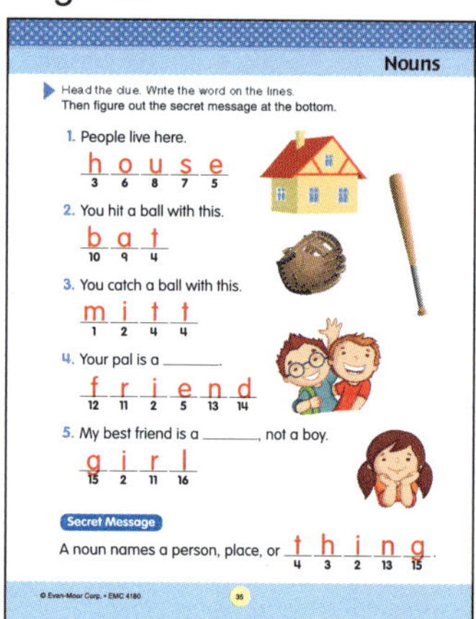

Nouns

Read the clue. Write the word on the lines. Then figure out the secret message at the bottom.

1. People live here. h o u s e
2. You hit a ball with this. b a t
3. You catch a ball with this. m i t t
4. Your pal is a ______. f r i e n d
5. My best friend is a ______, not a boy. g i r l

Secret Message

A noun names a person, place, or t h i n g.

Page 36

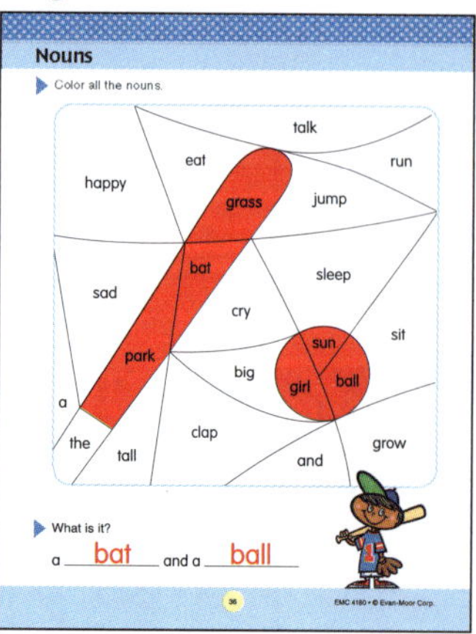

Nouns

Color all the nouns.

What is it?

a bat and a ball

Page 38

Verbs

Look at the picture. Use words from the box to finish the sentences.

jumped kicked broke ate

1. The goats ate the farmer's flowers.
2. When they saw him, they jumped over the fence.
3. One goat broke the farmer's fence.
4. Another goat kicked its heels with joy.

Page 39

Verbs

Read the story. Circle the verbs in the story.

What a mess! Toby escaped again. He chased the neighbor's cat. He spilled trash and trampled the flowers. He barked. He ran here and there. Oh, Toby!

Page 40

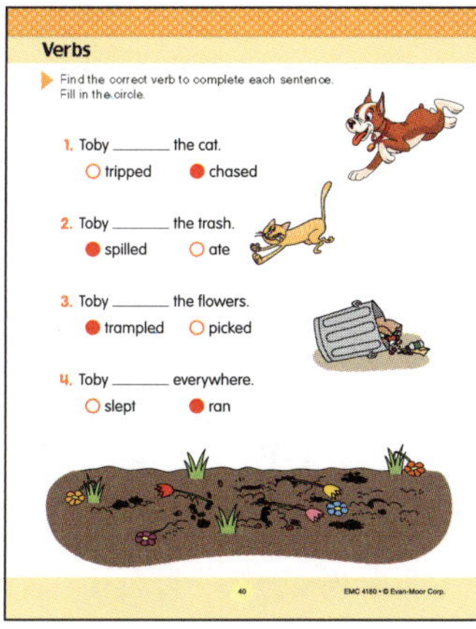

Page 41

Page 42

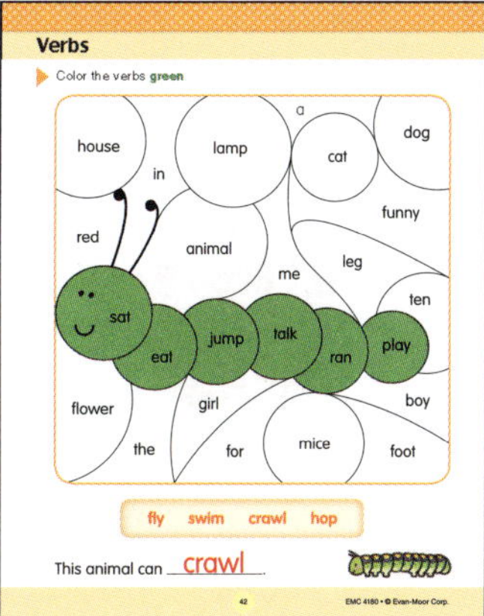

Page 44

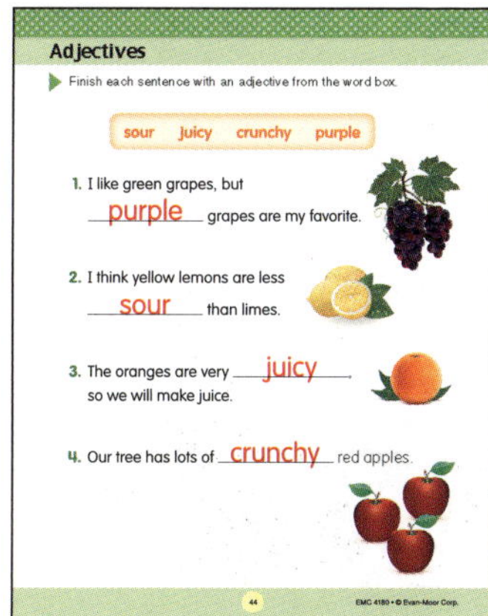

Page 45

Page 46

Page 47

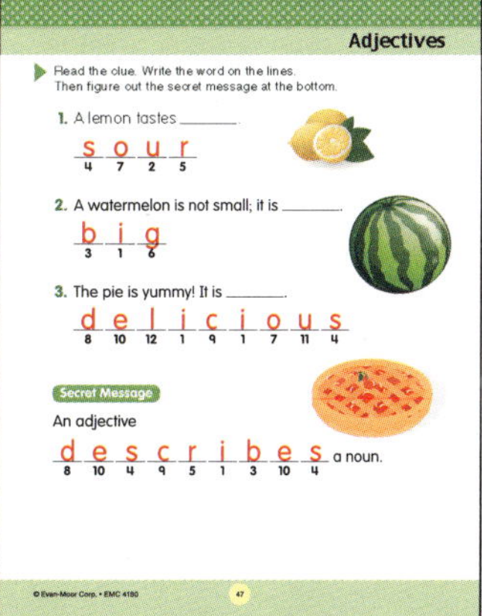

Page 48

Page 49

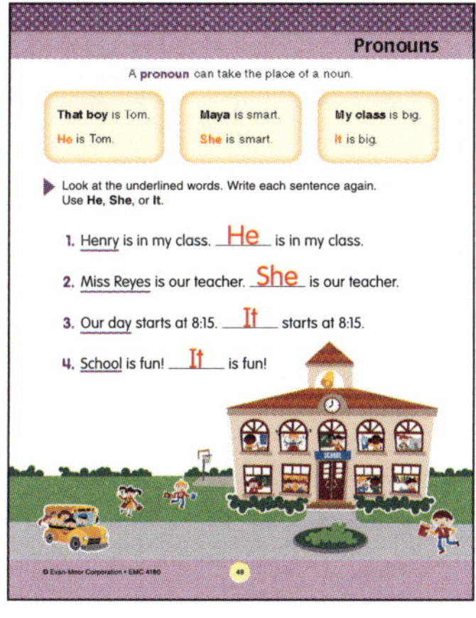

Page 50

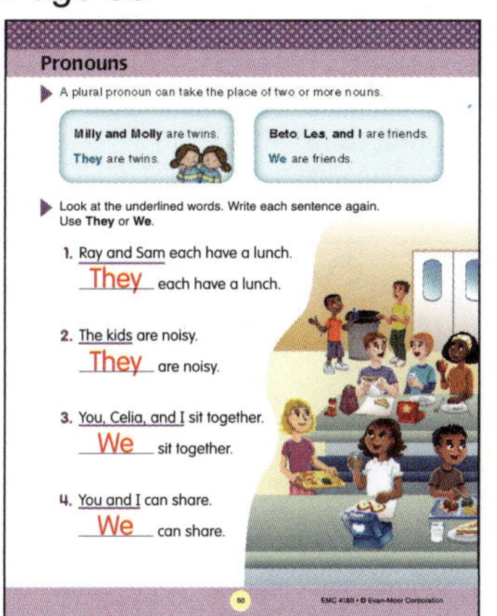

Page 51

Page 52

Page 53

Pronouns

Read the story. Circle the pronouns in the story.

I have lots of friends in school. First, there is Emily. I like her. We sit together at lunch. She is smart and she helps me to read. Sam is nice to me too. He plays baseball. He has played it since first grade. We play ball at recess with Ryan, Cory, and Sofia. They are good friends too.

Page 54

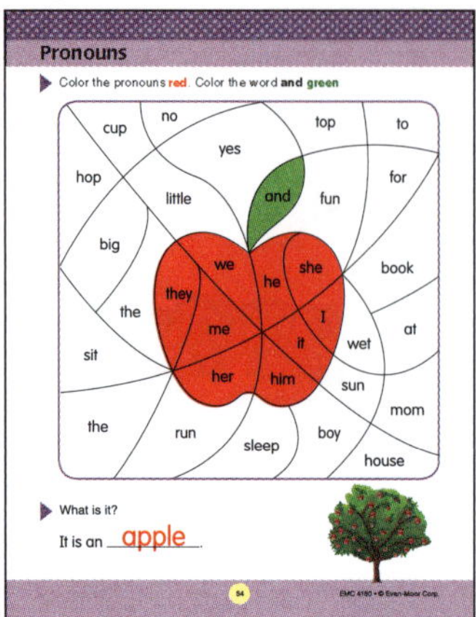
Pronouns

Color the pronouns red. Color the word and green.

What is it?

It is an apple

Page 56

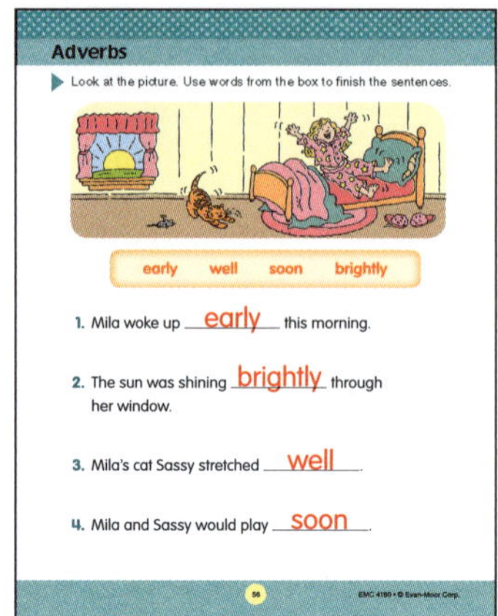
Adverbs

Look at the picture. Use words from the box to finish the sentences.

early well soon brightly

1. Mila woke up early this morning.
2. The sun was shining brightly through her window.
3. Mila's cat Sassy stretched well
4. Mila and Sassy would play soon

Page 57

Adverbs

Read the story. A few action words are underlined. Adverbs tell how or when. Circle the adverbs.

Mila and Sassy visit the park often. Today was a good day. A butterfly landed gently on Mila's hand. Can you believe it? It crawled to the tip of Mila's finger and softly fluttered its wings. Mila smiled and watched it closely.

Page 58

Adverbs

Find the best adverb to complete each sentence. Fill in the circle.

1. Mila and Sassy ______ visit the park. often / never
2. A butterfly landed ______ on her hand. suddenly / gently
3. It fluttered its wings ______. softly / quickly
4. Mila watched the butterfly ______. closely / oddly

Page 59

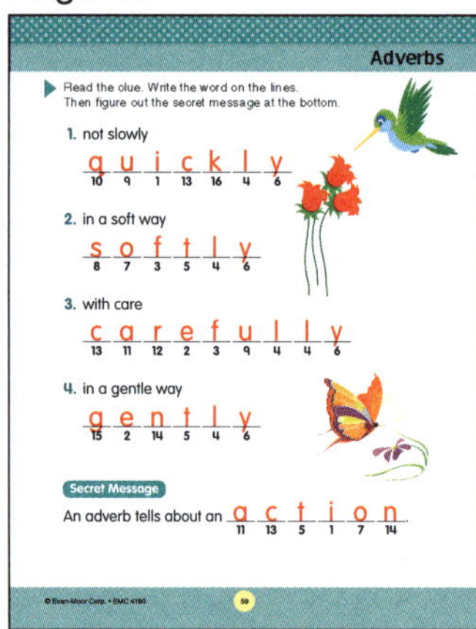
Adverbs

Read the clue. Write the word on the lines. Then figure out the secret message at the bottom.

1. not slowly — quickly
2. in a soft way — softly
3. with care — carefully
4. in a gentle way — gently

Secret Message

An adverb tells about an action

Page 60

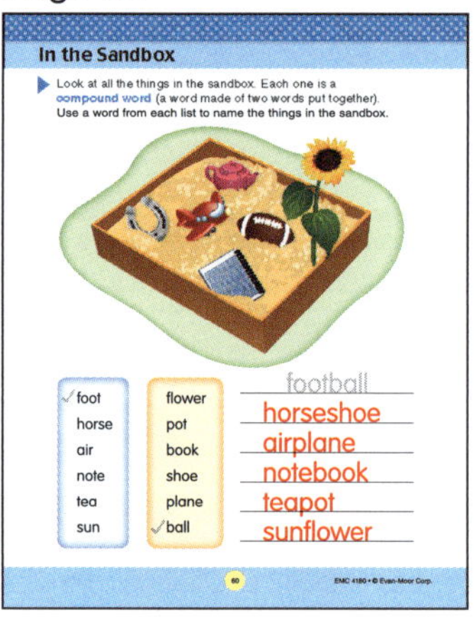
In the Sandbox

Look at all the things in the sandbox. Each one is a compound word (a word made of two words put together). Use a word from each list to name the things in the sandbox.

foot	flower
horse	pot
air	book
note	shoe
tea	plane
sun	ball

football
horseshoe
airplane
notebook
teapot
sunflower

Page 61

Rainy Day Compounds

Use words from both clouds to make compound words. Label the picture.

back lunch rain side — box coat pack walk

backpack raincoat lunchbox sidewalk

Complete each compound word.

rain bow
rain drops
rain fall
rain coat

Page 62

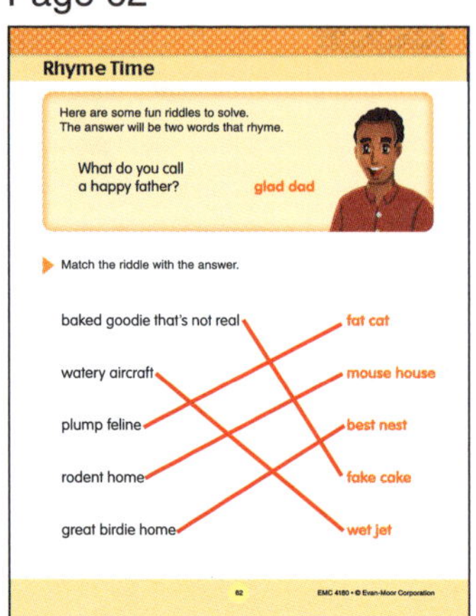
Rhyme Time

Here are some fun riddles to solve. The answer will be two words that rhyme.

What do you call a happy father? glad dad

Match the riddle with the answer.

baked goodie that's not real — fake cake
watery aircraft — wet jet
plump feline — fat cat
rodent home — mouse house
great birdie home — best nest

Page 63

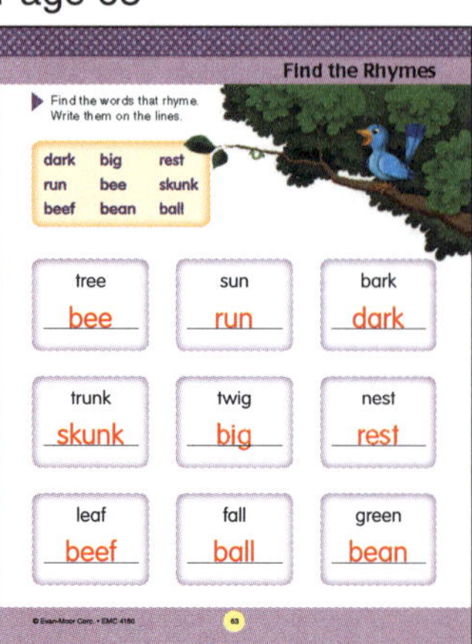
Find the Rhymes

Find the words that rhyme. Write them on the lines.

dark big rest
run bee skunk
beef bean ball

tree — bee	sun — run	bark — dark
trunk — skunk	twig — big	nest — rest
leaf — beef	fall — ball	green — bean

Page 64

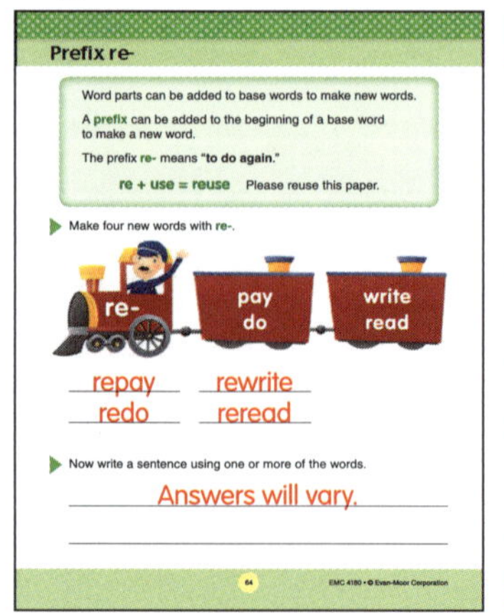
Prefix re-

Word parts can be added to base words to make new words.

A prefix can be added to the beginning of a base word to make a new word.

The prefix re- means "to do again."

re + use = reuse Please reuse this paper.

Make four new words with re-.

re- pay do write read

repay rewrite
redo reread

Now write a sentence using one or more of the words.

Answers will vary.

Page 65

Prefixes mis- and dis-

The prefixes mis- and dis- both mean "not."

Answer these clues. Use the word box to help you.

disobey misspell dishonest misdial disbelieve

to write a word wrong misspell
to get a wrong number misdial
to not believe disbelieve
not honest dishonest
to not obey disobey

Why is the girl angry?

Because her dog misbehaves

Page 66

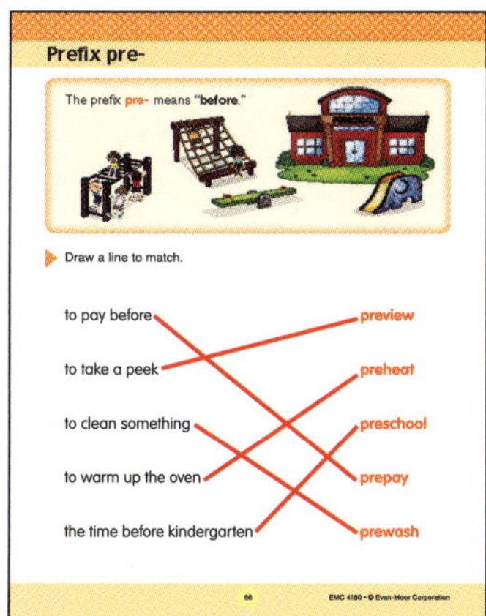

Page 67

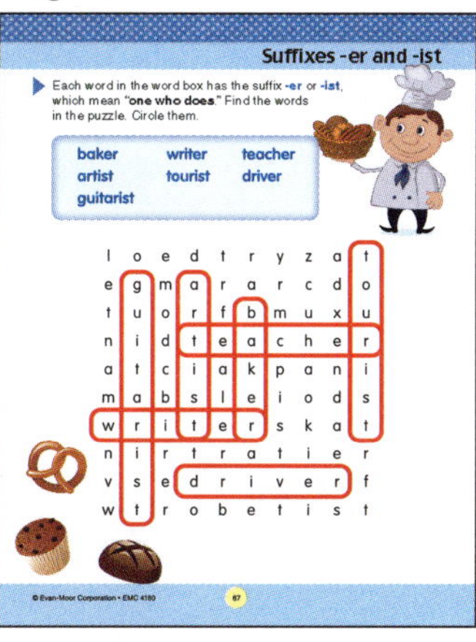

Page 68

Page 69

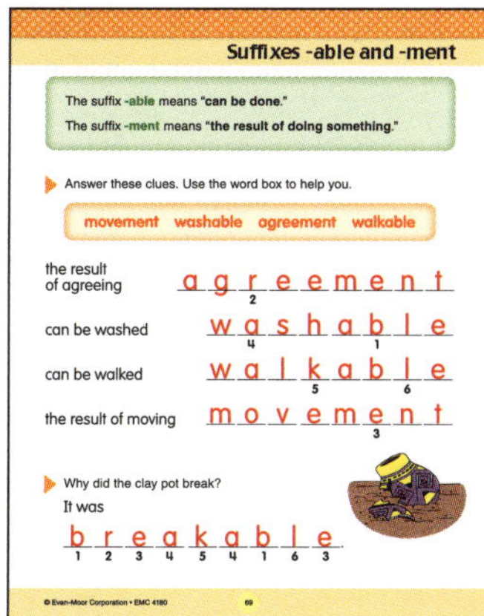

Page 70

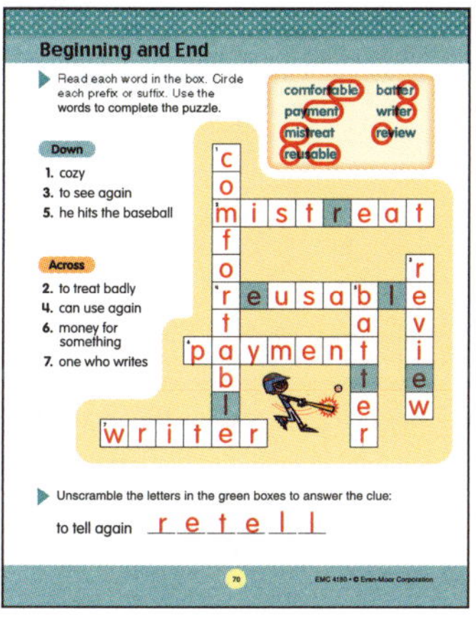

Page 71

Page 72

Page 73

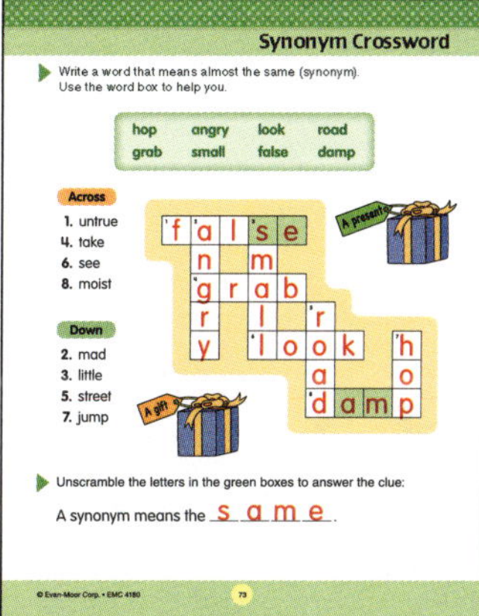

Page 74

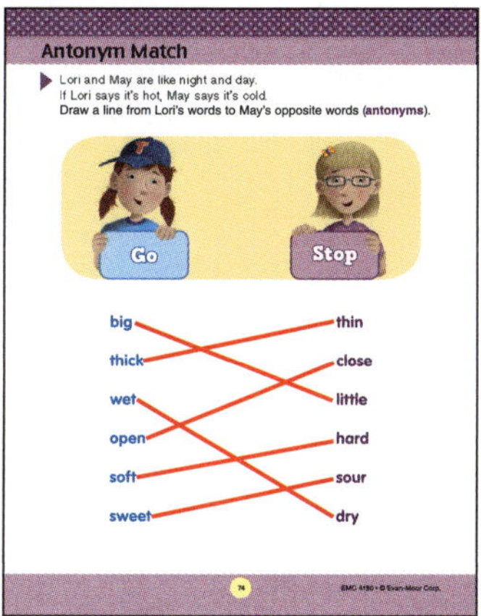

Page 75

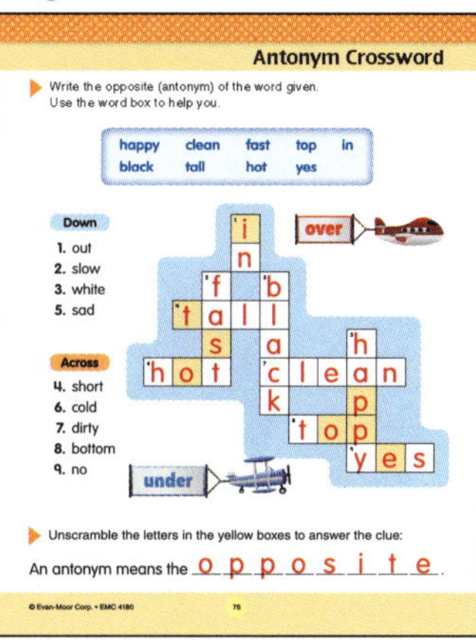

Page 76

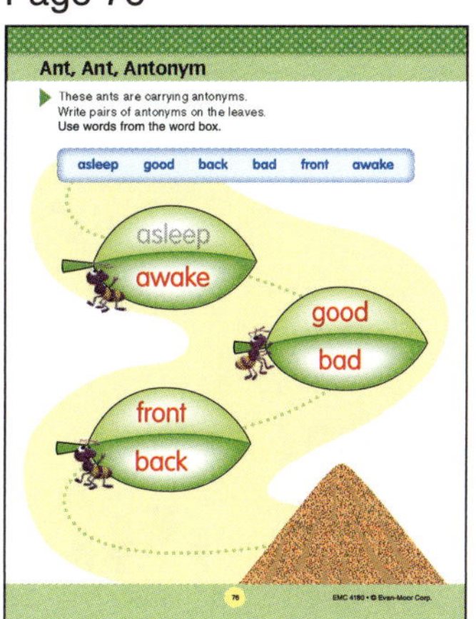

Page 77

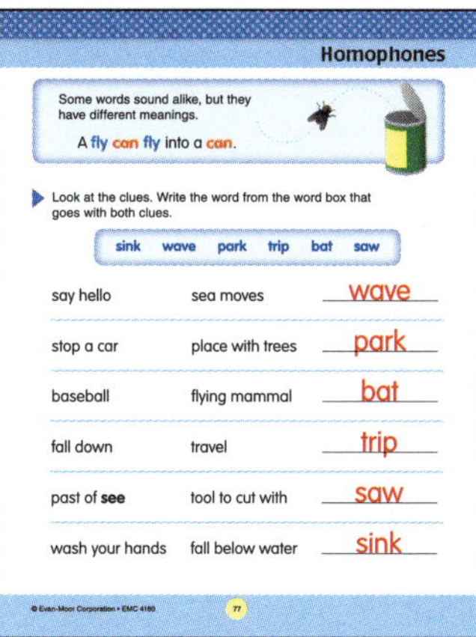

Page 78

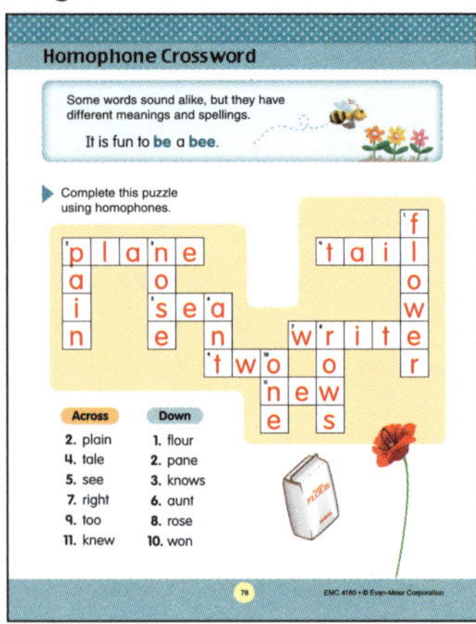
Homophone Crossword

Some words sound alike, but they have different meanings and spellings.

It is fun to be a bee.

Complete this puzzle using homophones.

Across
2. plain
4. tale
5. see
7. right
9. too
11. knew

Down
1. flour
2. pane
3. knows
6. aunt
8. rose
10. won

Page 79

Telephone Homophones

Find the homophones in the telephone. Circle them. Use the word boxes to help you.

BEAT BEET | MAIN MANE | MAIL MALE | SO SEW | PIECE PEACE

Page 80

There, They're, Their

There, they're, and their are homophones.

See my grandparents over there?

They're here for a week.

I'm their only grandchild.

Write there, they're, or their. Then read the poem aloud.

My grandparents are a grand pair.

They always take me here and there

Their house is not far.

We travel by car.

They're taking me now to the fair!

Page 81

It's, Its

It's means "it is."
It is raining. It's raining.

Its shows possession.
The tree lost its leaves.

Write it's or its. Then read the poem aloud.

It's raining.

It's pouring.

It's time to go exploring.

A bird is in its nest

And it will do its best

To keep its babies dry

This wet and windy morning.

Page 82

You're, Your

You're means "you are."
You are my best friend.
You're my best friend.

Your shows possession.
Here is your gift.

Write you're or your. Then sing the song to the tune of "Happy Birthday."

It's your big day. Hooray!

You're a good friend, I say.

All your pals are together.

And you're going to play!

Page 83

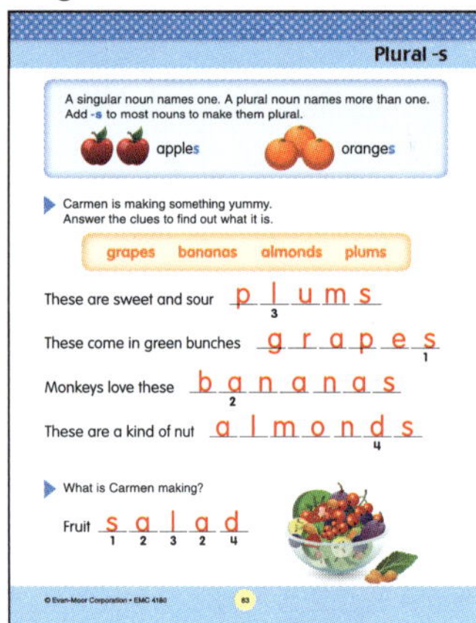
Plural -s

A singular noun names one. A plural noun names more than one. Add -s to most nouns to make them plural.

apples oranges

Carmen is making something yummy. Answer the clues to find out what it is.

grapes bananas almonds plums

These are sweet and sour p l u m s

These come in green bunches g r a p e s

Monkeys love these b a n a n a s

These are a kind of nut a l m o n d s

What is Carmen making?

Fruit s a l a d

Page 84

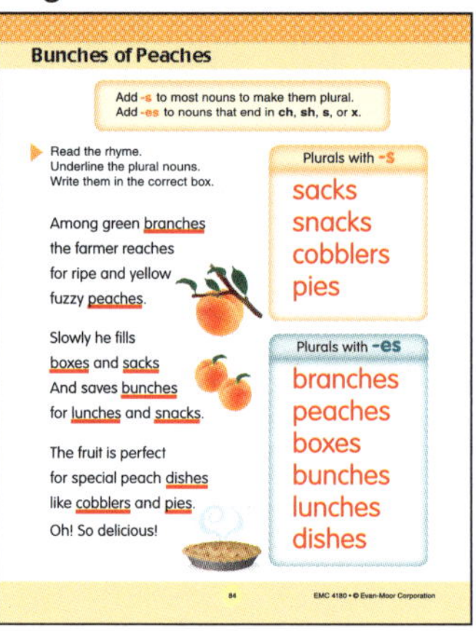
Bunches of Peaches

Add -s to most nouns to make them plural.
Add -es to nouns that end in ch, sh, s, or x.

Read the rhyme.
Underline the plural nouns.
Write them in the correct box.

Among green branches
the farmer reaches
for ripe and yellow
fuzzy peaches.

Slowly he fills
boxes and sacks
And saves bunches
for lunches and snacks.

The fruit is perfect
for special peach dishes
like cobblers and pies.
Oh! So delicious!

Plurals with -s: sacks, snacks, cobblers, pies

Plurals with -es: branches, peaches, boxes, bunches, lunches, dishes

Page 85

Babies and Butterflies

Some nouns end in a consonant + y.
Change the y to i and add -es to make the plural.
sky ⟶ skies

Answer the clues. Use the word box to help you.

lady butterfly puppy kitty baby

cats k i t t i e s

young dogs p u p p i e s

young people b a b i e s

___ and gentlemen l a d i e s

insects b u t t e r f l i e s

Where can you find all these?

in a p a r k

Page 86

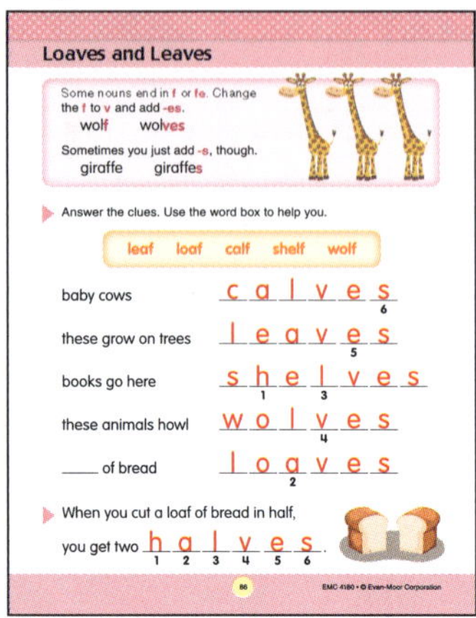
Loaves and Leaves

Some nouns end in f or fe. Change the f to v and add -es.
wolf wolves

Sometimes you just add -s, though.
giraffe giraffes

Answer the clues. Use the word box to help you.

leaf loaf calf shelf wolf

baby cows c a l v e s

these grow on trees l e a v e s

books go here s h e l v e s

these animals howl w o l v e s

___ of bread l o a v e s

When you cut a loaf of bread in half, you get two h a l v e s

Page 87

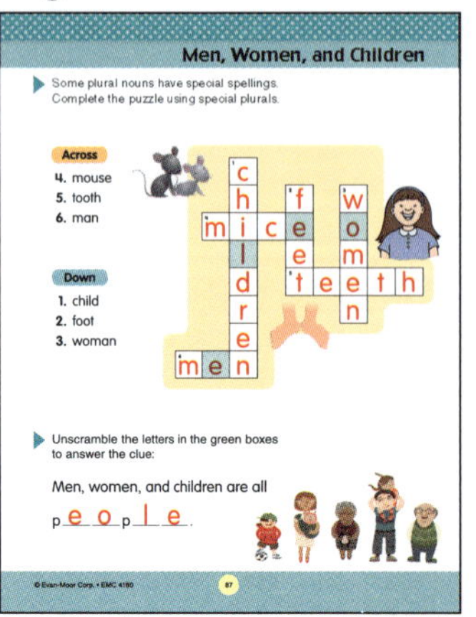
Men, Women, and Children

Some plural nouns have special spellings. Complete the puzzle using special plurals.

Across
4. mouse
5. tooth
6. man

Down
1. child
2. foot
3. woman

Unscramble the letters in the green boxes to answer the clue:

Men, women, and children are all

p e o p l e

Page 88

One Fish, Two Fish

Some special nouns are spelled the same in both singular and plural.

Read the poem. Decide if the underlined noun is singular or plural. If it is singular, circle it in green. If it is plural, circle it in blue.

A tired sheep

Fast asleep,

Saw three red fish

Swish, swish, swish.

Two big moose

Were drinking juice.

And a baby deer

Was standing near.

Page 89

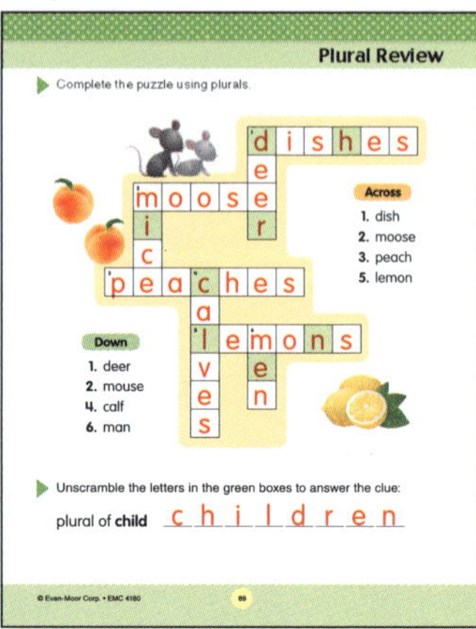
Plural Review

Complete the puzzle using plurals.

Across
1. dish
2. moose
3. peach
5. lemon

Down
1. deer
2. mouse
4. calf
6. man

Unscramble the letters in the green boxes to answer the clue:

plural of child c h i l d r e n